$\mathcal{D}$

b

to ~~you~~

Pastor Minnick. I've only started
reading my copy. LORD bless you
my friend & may HE give you the
Triumphing over Grace & peace
to cast out all fear
Sinful fear & put your TRUST in HIM alone!

Love, Kathy W. Oliver

ins
~~ent~~
by

SERIES EDITORS
Joel R. Beeke & Jay T. Collier

Interest in the Puritans continues to grow, but many people find the reading of these giants of the faith a bit unnerving. This series seeks to overcome that barrier by presenting Puritan books that are convenient in size and unintimidating in length. Each book is carefully edited with modern readers in mind, smoothing out difficult language of a bygone era while retaining the meaning of the original authors. Books for the series are thoughtfully selected to provide some of the best counsel on important subjects that people continue to wrestle with today.

Triumphing over Sinful Fear

John Flavel

Edited by
J. Stephen Yuille

Reformation Heritage Books
Grand Rapids, Michigan

Triumphing over Sinful Fear
© 2011 by Reformation Heritage Books

Published by
Reformation Heritage Books
2965 Leonard St., NE
Grand Rapids, MI 49525
616-977-0889 / Fax: 616-285-3246
e-mail: orders@heritagebooks.org
website: www.heritagebooks.org

Printed in the United States of America
18 19 20 21 22 23/11 10 9 8 7 6 5 4

Originally published as *A Practical Treatise of Fear* (London, 1682).
Special thanks to Mark E. Langenbach for supplying an electronic
copy of the text.

Library of Congress Cataloging-in-Publication Data

Flavel, John, 1630?-1691.
  [Practical treatise of fear]
  Triumphing over sinful fear / John Flavel ; edited by J. Stephen
Yuille.
      p. cm. — (Puritan treasures for today)
  "Originally published as A practical treatise of fear (London,
1682)"—T.p. verso.
  ISBN 978-1-60178-132-1 (pbk. : alk. paper) 1. Fear—Religious
aspects—Christianity—Early works to 1800. 2. Fear of God—
Christianity—Early works to 1800. 3. Christian life—Presbyterian
authors. I. Yuille, J. Stephen, 1968- II. Title. III. Series.
  BV4908.5.F63 2011
  241'.31—dc22
                                        2011015761

---

*For additional Reformed literature, both new and used, request a free book
list from Reformation Heritage Books at the above address.*

Table of Contents

Preface

Years ago, my wife and I had the opportunity to visit Victoria Falls, Zimbabwe. On the spur of the moment, we decided to go kayaking. Our guide organized a breakfast for us on the banks of the beautiful Zambezi River. He then provided a brief training session, followed by a stern warning: "This is a wild river. You'll have no problem with the crocodiles, as long as you remain in your kayak. But the hippos are another matter entirely. If they feel threatened by you, they'll strike from below." He proceeded to snap a twig and announced (with what I think was a twinkle in his eye): "A hippo will vaporize your kayak!" I was ready to back out, but the peer pressure was too great. And so we proceeded on our kayaking adventure. It was delightful until near the end of the trip, when we entered a narrow stretch in the river. Suddenly, four sets of eyes appeared on the surface of the water.

According to John Flavel, what I experienced at that moment is known as natural fear: "The trouble or perturbation of mind, from the comprehension of approaching evil or impending danger." For Flavel, such fear is an essential part of human nature (a key to survival), because we fear what threatens us, and, in response, we avoid what we fear.

That definition is simple enough, but Flavel does not stop there. He proceeds to explain that natural fear can quickly turn into sinful fear. That happens when fear springs from "unbelief, and an unworthy distrust of God." In other words, natural fear becomes sinful fear when we fail to trust God's promises in the face of danger. Now, in speaking of danger, Flavel is not primarily concerned with hippos (although I am sure it applies on some level), but people—wicked people. He knows that Christians experience persecution and he knows that they are tempted to "distrust" God, thereby succumbing to sinful fear when the suffering associated with persecution looms large.

Such temptation is not a matter of mere conjecture for Flavel. On the contrary, he writes from experience. In 1662 in England, Parliament passed an Act of Uniformity, requiring ministers (who had not received Episcopal ordination) to be re-ordained. It also required ministers to declare their consent to the entire Book of Common Prayer and their rejection of the Solemn League and Covenant. The Church of England ejected those ministers (including Flavel) who refused to conform; they became known as dissenters or nonconformists. After his ejection from public ministry in the town of Dartmouth, Flavel continued to meet secretly with his former church members in order to preach the

Scriptures and administer the sacraments. But, when the Oxford Act prohibited all nonconformist ministers from living within five miles of towns that sent representatives to Parliament, Flavel was forced to move to a different village. His people still ventured to hear him preach in private homes or wooded areas; and he slipped regularly into Dartmouth to visit them. In 1687, the authorities finally permitted Flavel to resume preaching in public. He enjoyed this liberty until his death four years later at age sixty-four. This brief account of Flavel's ministry demonstrates that he was well-acquainted with persecution. He knew first-hand the ever-present danger of losing sight of God's promises and succumbing to sinful fear in the midst of suffering.

In this book Flavel handles this vital subject. He begins by examining the types and uses of fear in general. He then turns to sinful fear in particular, expounding its causes, effects, and remedies. In his chapter on remedies, he gives twelve "rules" for dealing with sinful fear. Interestingly, he states that the first eleven are "reducible" to the last: "Exalt the fear of God in your hearts, and let it gain the ascendant over all your other fears." In other words, the best cure for sinful fear is the fear of God.

Regrettably, many modern readers grow perplexed at the mere mention of the fear of God. They reject any notion that fear is to characterize the Christian's approach to God. After all, "There is no fear in love; but perfect love casteth out fear" (1 John 4:8a). However, in making this assertion, they fail to understand that there are two ways to fear God: a good way and a bad way. Flavel affirms this distinction, but he does not develop it in this book. Because of the potential confusion, it is worth turning for a moment to his fellow Puritans, who are very careful to distinguish between what George Swinnock calls filial and servile fear, what William Gurnall calls holy and slavish fear, or what Stephen Charnock calls reverential and bondage fear. In short, they are careful to affirm that there are two different ways to fear God: a good way and a bad way, a godly way and an ungodly way. Their distinction is biblical. When the Israelites gather at the base of Sinai, they see the fire, smoke, and lightning, and they hear the thunder. As a result, they are terrified. But Moses says to them, "Fear not: for God is come to prove you, and that his fear may be before your face, that ye sin not." It appears that Moses commands the Israelites both to fear God and not to fear God. How do we explain this apparent contradiction? "Mark it," says John Bunyan, "here are two fears: a fear forbidden and a fear commended."

Forbidden (or ungodly) fear arises from the mere threat of God's punishment. In the above example, the Israelites fear God because they view Him as a threat. They regard Him as hazardous to their well-being. But this kind of fear fails to make any lasting impression upon their souls. Gurnall explains, "Often we see God's judgments leave such an impression on men's spirits that for a while they stand aloof from their sins… but when they see fair weather continue, and no clouds gather towards another storm, they descend to their old wicked practices, and grow more bold and heaven-daring than ever." In short, forbidden fear is merely concerned with self-preservation. It does not take God's glory into account. On the contrary, it actually desires the removal of what it perceives as dangerous, meaning it desires the removal of God.

We find instances of such fear throughout Scripture. For example, in Moses' day, some of the Egyptian officials fear God. As a result, they bring their servants and cattle in from their fields in order to avoid the hailstorm. However, it is an ungodly fear. They are only concerned with avoiding the perceived threat. They are only concerned with alleviating the danger. A little later, Moses says to Pharaoh, "But as for thee and thy servants, I know that ye will not yet fear the LORD God." By way of another example, we read that the foreign inhabitants (transplanted by the king of Assyria after his invasion of Israel) fear God. They view Him as a potential source of harm, because He has sent lions among them to punish them for their idolatry. They commission one of the priests to instruct them in the worship of God. They go through the motions of worshipping Him, while continuing to serve their own idols. In brief, they take steps to minimize the perceived threat to their well-being while remaining steadfast in their sin and rebellion. That is the essence of ungodly (or forbidden) fear.

Commended (or godly) fear does not arise from a perception of God as hazardous, but glorious. In other words, it flows from an appreciation of God. According to William Gouge, it "arises from faith in the mercy and goodness of God." When the soul feels "a sweet taste of God's goodness" and finds "that in his favour only all happiness consists, it is stricken with such an inward awe and reverence." Such fear inclines the soul to love what God loves and hate what God hates. In simple terms, this means that commended fear (unlike forbidden fear) makes a divorce between sin and the soul. C. H. Spurgeon (who drank deeply from the Puritans) describes this "divorce" as follows:

> To a believing heart, God is all purity. His light is "as the color of the terrible crystal," of which Ezekiel writes. His brightness is so great that no man can approach unto it. We are so sinful that, when we get even a glimpse of the divine holiness, we are filled with fear, and we cry, with Job, "I have heard of Thee by the hearing of the ear: but now mine eye seeth Thee. Wherefore I abhor myself, and repent in dust and ashes." This is a kind of fear which we have need to cultivate, for it leads . to repentance, and confession of sin, to aspirations after holiness, and to the utter rejection of all self-complacency and self-conceit.

Here, Spurgeon identifies three marks of godly fear: (1) "repentance and confession of sin"; (2) "aspirations after holiness"; and (3) "the utter rejection of all self-complacency and self-conceit." All of this means that we are no longer lovers of self and haters of God, but lovers of God and haters of self. As a result, we surrender ourselves to God's will. Gouge provides a good summary: godly fear results in "a careful endeavour to please God" and "a careful avoiding of such things as offend the Majesty of God."

It is precisely this fear that Flavel has in mind in this book. He defines it as "a gracious habit or principle planted by God in the soul, whereby the soul is kept under a holy awe of the eye of God, and from thence is inclined to perform and do what pleases him, and to shun and avoid whatever he forbids and hates." For Flavel, this is a sure remedy for sinful fear. Knowing that Christians are prone to lose sight of God in the midst of suffering, he encourages them to look to the One whose power is "almighty," whose wisdom is "infinite and unsearchable," and whose love is "transcendent and unparalleled." When they do, they will find cause to trust Him in the midst of life's deepest trials.

J. Stephen Yuille
Glen Rose, Texas
October 2010

CHAPTER 1

Introduction

Say ye not, A confederacy, to all them to whom this people shall say, A confederacy; neither fear ye their fear, nor be afraid. Sanctify the LORD of hosts himself; and let him be your fear, and let him be your dread. And he shall be for a sanctuary.

—Isaiah 8:12–14a

There is as much diversity in people's inward moods and dispositions as in their outward features. Some are as frightened as rabbits and jump at every sound—even a dog's bark. Some are as bold as lions and face danger without trembling. Some fear more than they ought, some before they ought, and others when they ought not at all. The carnal person fears man, not God. The strong Christian fears God, not man. The weak Christian fears man too much and God too little.

There is a fear which is the effect of sin. It springs from guilt and hurries the soul into more guilt. There is a fear which is the effect of grace. It springs from our love for God and His interest and drives the soul to Him in the way of duty. The less fear a person has, the more happiness he has—unless, of course, it is that fear which is his happiness and excellence.

It cannot be said of any person, as it is said of Leviathan: he is "made without fear" (Job 41:33b). The strongest people are not without some fears. When the church is in the storms of persecution, and almost covered with the waves, her most courageous passengers may suffer as much from this boisterous passion within as from the storm without. This is the result of not thoroughly believing or seasonably remembering that the Lord—Admiral of all the oceans and Commander of all the winds—is on board the ship to steer and preserve it from the storm. A weighty example of this very thing is found in the context, where we discover that the best people tremble in expectation of the worst events—both on the church in general and themselves in particular: "And it was told the house of David, saying, Syria is confederate with Ephraim. And his heart was moved, and the heart of his people, as the trees of the wood are moved with the wind" (Isa. 7:2).

If their danger is measured by sense alone, then their fear does not exceed its cause. As a matter of fact, their danger seems to exceed their fear, for a foreign and cruel enemy (Assyria) is about to break upon them like a breach of the sea, and overflow the land of Immanuel: "Now, therefore, behold, the Lord bringeth up upon them the waters of the river, strong and many, even the king of Assyria, and all his glory: and he shall come up over all his channels and go over all his banks" (Isa. 8:7). This verse describes the enemy as "waters" that quickly drown the country upon which they break. The next verse tells us how far this enemy will prevail and how close the country will come to total ruin: "And he shall pass through Judah; he shall overflow and go over, he shall reach even to the neck; and the stretching out of his wings shall fill the breadth of thy land, O Immanuel" (Isa. 8:8). All the land, except the capital city, will be under water.

Having described the invading enemy's power and success, God derides their plots and schemes (Isa. 8:9–10). Although He permits them to afflict His people for a time, for His own just and holy ends, He assures them that the issue of all their counsels and cruelties will recoil upon them and result in their own ruin and confusion. He then commands Isaiah to encourage the feeble and trembling hearts of those who fear Him in the midst of those terrifying times: "For the LORD spake thus to me with a strong hand and instructed me that I should not walk in the way of this people, saying, Say ye not, A confederacy" (Isa. 8:11–12a).

Speaking to the prophet with a strong hand, God uses the mighty impression that the spirit of prophecy makes upon his heart. He lays, as it were, His hand upon him, as a person does upon one to whom he is about to impart some special secret in a familiar way. Drawing him close with a friendly hand, He says, "Come here, Isaiah. Take note of what I am about to entrust to you in respect to yourself and My elect people who follow you. Do not say, 'A confederacy,' to whomever this people say, 'A confederacy.' In other words, do not let these frightful tidings affect you the way they affect Ahaz and those with him. They are so terrified at the approaching danger that all their counsels, thoughts, and studies are occupied with preventing it. They seek an alliance with Assyria (Hos. 5:13). If that fails, then they will seek protection from some foreign power against Assyria. But their eyes do not look to Me for protection and deliverance. They expect more from Egypt than from heaven, more from a broken reed than from the Rock of Ages. Do not fear their fear! It drives them from Me to the creature. It first distracts them, and then ensnares them. In marked contrast, see that you and all the faithful in the land sanctify Me in your hearts, and make Me your fear and dread. Rely upon Me by faith in this day of trouble. See that you give Me the glory of My wisdom, power, and faithfulness by relying entirely upon My attributes that are engaged for you in so many tested promises. Do not give yourselves to sinful and vain dealings, as those who have no interest in Me nor experience of Me."

That is the text's general scope and design. In terms of its particulars, we find a sin condemned, a remedy prescribed, and a motive encouraged.

A Sin Condemned

"Neither fear ye their fear, nor be afraid" (Isa. 8:12b). This kind of fear is a sinful principle. It will incline them to do what their countrymen did, namely, to say "A confederacy." Sinful fear will cause the best people to attempt to help themselves through sinful compromises. This is the fear that plagues the carnal and unbelieving Jews. It enslaves them in bondage of spirit. It is the fruit of sin, a sin in its own nature, and the cause of much sin. It is God's just punishment upon them for their other sins. But Isaiah's listeners must not permit their fear to produce in them such negative effects. They must not forget God, magnify the creature, or prefer their own schemes and policies to God's almighty power and unchanging faithfulness.

A Remedy Prescribed

"Sanctify the LORD of hosts himself; and let him be your fear, and let him be your dread" (Isa. 8:13). The fear of God will swallow up the fear of man. A reverential awe and dread of God will extinguish the creature's slavish fear, as the rain puts out the fire. To sanctify the Lord of hosts is to acknowledge the glory of His sovereign power, wisdom, and faithfulness. It includes not only a verbal confession, but internal acts of trust, confidence, and entire dependence upon Him. These are our choicest respects towards God, and give Him the greatest glory. Moreover, they are the most beneficial and comfortable acts we perform for our own peace and safety in times of danger. If we look to God in the day of trouble, fear Him as the Lord of hosts (i.e., the One who governs all creatures and commands all the armies of heaven and earth), and rely upon His care and love as a child depends upon his father's protection, then we will know rest and peace. Who would be afraid to pass through the midst of armed troops and regiments, if he knew that the general was his own father? The more this filial fear has power over our hearts, the less we will dread the creature's power. When the dictator ruled at Rome, then all other officers ceased. Likewise, when the fear of God is dictator in the heart, all other fears will (in great measure) cease.

A Motive Encouraged

"And he shall be for a sanctuary" (Isa. 8:14a). If we sanctify the Lord of hosts by acknowledging Him and depending upon Him in times of danger, then He will be our sanctuary. He will surely protect, defend, and provide for us in the worst times and cases. "And the LORD will create upon every dwelling place of mount Zion, and upon her assemblies, a cloud and smoke by day, and the shining of a flaming fire by night: for upon all the glory shall be a defense. And there shall be a tabernacle for a shadow in the daytime from the heat, and for a place of refuge, and for a covert from storm and from rain" (Isa. 4:5–6). Let the wind roar, the rain beat, the lightning flash, we are in safety and have a good roof over our heads.

Conclusion

Two points of doctrine emerge from the above explanation of the text. First, the best people are easily overcome with slavish fear in times of imminent distress and danger. Second, the fear of God is the most effectual means for extinguishing sinful fear and keeping us from danger. These two doctrines capture the scope and substance of the text. In the following chapters, I will not belabor them, but focus my attention on the types, uses, causes, effects, and remedies of fear.

CHAPTER 2

Types of Fear

There is a threefold fear in humanity: natural, sinful, and religious.

Natural Fear

Everyone experiences natural fear. It is the trouble or agitation of mind that arises when we perceive approaching evil or impending danger. It is not always sinful, but it is always the fruit and consequence of sin. Ever since sin entered human nature, it has been impossible to shake off this fear. As soon as Adam transgressed, he feared, hiding himself "amongst the trees of the garden" (Gen. 3:8b). When he transgressed the covenant, he immediately feared the execution of the curse. First, he eats; then, he hides. He transmitted this afflictive passion to all his children.

It pleased our Lord Jesus Christ to subject Himself to natural fear, in the days of His flesh. He was afraid — even "sore amazed" (Mark 14:33). Although His human nature was absolutely free from sin, He came in the "likeness of sinful flesh" (Rom. 8:3).

This fear creates great trouble and agitation in the mind: "fear hath torment" (1 John 4:18). The agitation of the mind is proportionate to the fear, which, in turn, is proportionate to the perceived danger. When fear is exceedingly great, reason is displaced and unable to guide us. We become like sailors in a storm, whom the psalmist describes as "at their wits' end" (Ps. 107:27b). This is the meaning of Deuteronomy 28:25, "The LORD shall cause thee to be smitten before thine enemies: thou shalt go out one way against them, and flee seven ways before them: and shalt be removed into all the kingdoms of the earth." In other words, their fear and distraction are so great that they attempt to flee one way, then another, striving every way, but liking none. Their fear impedes the aid of reason to such an extent that their counsels are always uncertain and at a loss. A person's usual cry in this condition is this: "I do not know what to do. I do not know which way to turn."

Evil is the object of fear—the greater the evil, the stronger the fear. For this reason, the terrors of an awakened conscience are the greatest terrors. In this case, people deal with a great and terrible God. They are scared with apprehensions of His infinite and eternal wrath. No evil is greater than that. Christ's conflict with it was so great that it made Him sweat, as it were, great drops of blood. Death is the greatest of all temporal evils;

therefore, Job calls it the "king of terrors" (Job 18:14b). Jacque August de Thous, a French historian, relates two strange instances of the fear of death. The first is of a captain, who was so terrified with the fear of death that a bloody sweat poured out from every part of his body. The second is of a young man, whom Pope Sixtus V condemned to death for a trivial matter. He was so terrified at the prospect of death that he shed bloody tears. These are strange and terrible effects of fear, yet vastly short of what Christ suffered. He grappled with a far greater evil than the terrors of death; namely, the pouring out of God's wrath fully and immediately upon Him.

Evil is the principal object of hatred. However, when evil is imminent, it also provokes fear. The saints in glory are perfectly free from fear, because they are beyond the reach of all danger. We, on the other hand, are in the midst of all kinds of evil. We do not fear them, until we see them approaching, and are uncertain how to avoid them. To hear of fire, plague, or sword, in a foreign country does not frighten us because the evil is so remote. It is so far away that we are in no danger. However, when it is in our town or (even worse) in our home, we tremble. Evil does not hurt us through our mere apprehension of it, but our experience of it. It is worth observing that all carnal security is maintained by putting evil at a great distance from us. It is said of secure sensualists: they "put far away the evil day" (Amos 6:3a). This does not mean that they put the evil day farther away from them in reality, but only in their imagination. They shut their eyes and refuse to see it, lest it should interrupt their happiness. This is the reason why death does not frighten the living: it is apprehended as remote—at an undetermined distance. If the precise time of death were known (especially if that time were near), it would terrify them.

This fear is the affliction of nature. We all groan under its effects. It is in all creatures to some degree, but most prevalent in people. It makes them their own tormentors. When it prevails in a high degree upon us, it is the greatest of torments. Indeed, not all constitutions and temperaments experience the same degree of fear. Some people are naturally bold and courageous; they are like the lion in bravery and fortitude. Some people are exceedingly cowardly and faint-hearted; they are like the deer or rabbit—one little dog will make a hundred of them flee. Martin Luther was a man of great courage and presence of mind in the midst of danger. Philip Melanchthon, on the other hand, was very fearful and subject to despondency. The difference between them is expressed in one of Luther's letters to Melanchthon: "I am a secure spectator of things. I do not fear anything those fierce and threatening papists say. I dislike those anxious cares, which (as you write) almost consume you." There might be as much grace in one as in the other, but Melanchthon's grace did not have the advantage of Luther's bold and courageous temperament of body and mind.

Sinful Fear

There is a fear that is formally and intrinsically sinful. It is not only our unhappiness, but our fault. It is not only our affliction and burden, but our great evil and provocation. Such is the fear cautioned against in our text, where it is called "their fear" (Isa. 8:12). When dangers threaten, carnal and unbelieving people experience this fear. Its sinfulness lies in five things.

Its Cause

Sinful fear arises from unbelief—an unworthy distrust of God. This occurs when we fail to rely upon the security of God's promise; in other words, when we refuse to trust in God's protection. This was the case with Israel. "For thus saith the Lord GOD, the Holy One of Israel; In returning and rest shall ye be saved; in quietness and in confidence shall be your strength: and ye would not. But ye said, No; for we will flee upon horses; therefore shall ye flee: and, We will ride upon the swift; therefore shall they that pursue you be swift. One thousand shall flee at the rebuke of one" (Isa. 30:15–17a). The situation here is as follows. Sennacherib, along with a mighty army, is ready to invade Israel. This frightens the people. In their distress, God assures them through His prophet that in "returning and rest" they will be saved, and in "quietness and confidence" they will be strengthened. This means that they must not involve themselves with counsels and schemes designed to secure them under the wings of Egypt or some other protector. On the contrary, they must rest upon God's power with a calm, quiet, and composed state of mind. They must take His promises for their security. This will be their salvation and strength—more effective to their preservation than armies, garrisons, or any other defense in the world. In a word, one act of faith will do them more good than Pharaoh and all his forces. But they refuse to trust God. They decide that a good horse will do them more service than a good promise. They think Egypt offers them better security than heaven. This is the fruit of gross infidelity. Wicked people forsake God and cleave to the creature in times of trouble.

Some of this same distrust is found in the best people. It was in the disciples. Christ asks them, "Why are ye fearful, O ye of little faith?" (Matt. 8:26). A storm arises at sea. Danger begins to threaten them. Suddenly, their fear is more boisterous than the wind. It has more need of calming than the sea. It arises from their unbelief—the less their faith, the greater their fear.

If we were to rely upon God's promise (so far as He enables us to believe), we would reckon ourselves to be very secure. Matthias Flacius Illyricus, a Lutheran reformer, relates a remarkable account of Andreas Proles, an aged and godly divine, who lived a little before Luther. He taught many points of doctrine soundly, according to the light available to him at that time. Having been called to a Synod at Milan, he opposed the pope's proposal to institute a new church holiday as an unnecessary burden. As a result of his opposition, his life was in danger. After escaping, he bought weapons to protect himself. However, one day, as he was riding, he remembered that the cause belongs to God. It was not to be maintained with sword and bow. What could a decrepit old man do with weapons anyway? Soon after, he threw them away and committed his journey to God. He relied upon God's promises more than sword or bow. He returned home safely and, years later, died quietly in his bed.

Its Excess

The sinfulness of fear lies in its excess and immoderacy when we fear more than we ought. We might say of our fear, as the philosopher says of water, "It is hard to keep it within bounds." Every bush is a bear. Every petty trouble frightens us. Our fear exceeds the value and merit of its cause. It is a great sin to love or fear any creature above its worth, as if it were master of all our temporal and eternal comforts. When the people of Israel hear of their enemies' alliance against them, their hearts are moved "as the trees of the wood are moved with the wind" (Isa. 7:2b). It is a sad sight to see people shaking and quivering like trees on a windy day. Yet that is what the house of David does—partly because of their remembrance of past calamities, but especially because of their unbelief in God's protecting care in their present and future dangers.

This is too often the fault of good people in crea-
ture-fear and creature-love—they transgress the due
bounds of moderation. It is noted of Jacob that he was a
man of much faith. He had the sweetest encouragement
to strengthen it—both from former experiences and
from God's gracious promises. Yet, when Esau draws
near, he is "greatly afraid and distressed" (Gen. 32:7a).
Moments earlier, God had graciously appeared to him,
and sent a royal guard of angels to attend him (Gen.
32:1–2). Despite this encouraging vision, he is greatly
afraid and distressed as soon as Esau approaches.

Its Inordinacy

The sinfulness of our fear lies in its excessivness. To
fear something more than we ought is bad enough, but
to magnify its power above that of a creature is sinful.
When we exalt a creature's power by fearing it, we give it
ascendancy over us. In effect, we act as if it had arbitrary
and absolute dominion over us and our comforts—to
do with them whatever it pleases. In so doing, we elevate
the creature beyond its class and rank to the place of
God. This is a very sinful and evil fear.

To trust in any creature as if it had God's power to
help us, or to fear any creature as if it had God's power
to hurt us, is exceedingly sinful. It provokes God. He
condemns such inordinate trust in our text. The people
of Israel want to turn to Egypt for help. They trust in
their horses and horsemen because they are strong. In
their opinion, Egypt is able to secure them against all

that God declares through the prophet. To turn them from their sinful and inordinate dependence upon the creature, He warns them: "Now the Egyptians are men, and not God; and their horses flesh, and not spirit. When the LORD shall stretch out his hand, both he that helpeth shall fall, and he that is holpen shall fall down, and they all shall fail together" (Isa. 31:3). It is a sinful and dangerous mistake to give to a creature that trust and dependence that belongs to God alone. To look upon people as if they were gods, and horses as if they were spirits, is sinful. All creatures, even the strongest, are like the vine or ivy. If they clasp the pole, wall, or oak, they find support. But if they entangle themselves with one another, like the Israelites with the Egyptians, they all fall down.

We are inclined to a sinful trust and dependence upon each other, and to an inordinate fear and dread of each other. We act as if the creature were a god rather than a man, a spirit rather than flesh. Thus, our fear magnifies and exalts the creature, putting it (as it were) in God's room and place. God rebukes this sin in His own people: "I, even I, am he that comforteth you: Who art thou, that thou shouldest be afraid of a man that shall die, and of the son of man which shall be made as grass; and forgettest the LORD thy maker?" (Isa. 51:12–13a). It is evident that fear exalts people and belittles God. It thinks upon a person's hamful power so much that it forgets God's saving power. In this way, a mortal worm, which perishes as the grass, eclipses the glory of the great God, who stretched forth the heavens and laid the foundations of the earth.

Christ cautions His disciples against this evil: "And fear not them which kill the body, but are not able to kill the soul: but rather fear him which is able to destroy both soul and body in hell" (Matt. 10:28). Be careful not to fear any man, as if the power of making or marring you were in his hands—as if it were his will and pleasure to save or ruin you. Do not fear those who can only touch your body, as if they could damn your soul; do not attribute to any creature God's sovereign and incommunicable power.

Its Influence

The sinfulness of fear consists in the distracting influence it has upon the heart, whereby it unfits us for the discharge of our duties. At times, fear puts people into such a frenzy, and their thoughts into such disorder, that they receive little support or relief from their graces or from their reason. Under extraordinary fear, both grace and reason, like the wheels of a watch wound above its due height, stand still and have no motion at all.

It is rare to find a man of such constancy of heart and mind in a day of fear as Jehoshaphat. "Then there came some that told Jehoshaphat, saying, There cometh a great multitude against thee from beyond the sea on this side Syria; and, behold, they be in Hazazonta-mar, which is Engedi. And Jehoshaphat feared, and set himself to seek the LORD" (2 Chron. 20:2–3a). He "set himself," meaning he fixed and composed his heart for prayer in a time of great fright and terrible alarm. It is rare to find such constancy and evenness of mind. Most people are like those whom the prophet describes: when the enemy besieges Jerusalem, the people's joy turns to panic (Isa. 22:2–3). The city becomes tumultuous. Some people run to the tops of their houses, either to hide or mourn. The mere apprehension of misery kills many before the enemy's sword touches any. None of them run into their closets to seek God. The city is full of "stirs," but not of prayers. Fear makes them cry to the mountains rather than God (Isa. 22:5). The best people find it difficult to keep their thoughts from wandering and their minds from distraction in the greatest calm. It is a thousand times more difficult in the tumult of fear.

Its Power

The sinfulness of fear consists in its power to dispose and incline people to use sinful means to escape danger. This casts them into the hands of temptation. "The fear of man bringeth a snare" (Prov. 29:25a). Satan spreads the net and fear drives people right into it. Fear led Abraham, a great believer, into the snare of deception. This resulted in the great discredit of religion, for it was a strange sight to see Abimelech, a heathen, rebuking Abraham (Gen. 20:9). God rebukes His people for this same evil: "And of whom hast thou been afraid or feared, that thou hast lied, and hast not remembered me?"

(Isa. 57:11a). Fear leads to a double lie: one in words and one in deeds. Hypocrisy is a lie in deeds—a practical lie. The history of the church abounds with sad examples of deception through fear. It is Satan's great weapon to make his temptations victorious over men.

Religious Fear

There is a holy and laudable fear, which is our treasure, not our torment. It is the chief ornament of the soul—its beauty and perfection, not its unhappiness or sin. Natural fear is a pure and simple passion of the soul. Sinful fear is the disordered and corrupt passion of the soul. But the awful, filial fear of God is the natural passion sanctified—changed and baptized into the name and nature of a spiritual grace. This fear is also mentioned in our text. It is prescribed as an antidote against sinful fear. It devours carnal fear, as Moses' serpent devoured those of the enchanters (Ex. 7:12). Living night and day in the fear of man is one of the worst judgments (Deut. 28:65–67), but living "all the day long" in the fear of God is one of the sweetest mercies (Prov. 23:17). The fear of man shortens our days, but the fear of God prolongs them (Prov. 10:27). The fear of man is a fountain of mischief and misery, but the fear of God is a fountain of life (Prov. 14:27). The fear of man causes people to run to evil (Prov. 29:25), but the fear of God causes them to depart from evil (Prov. 16:6).

This fear is a gracious habit or principle, which God plants in the soul, whereby it is kept under a holy awe of the eye of God. As a result, it is inclined to do what pleases God and avoid what He forbids and hates. There are four parts to this definition. (1) God plants this fear in the soul as a fixed and permanent habit. It is not, therefore, a natural product of our heart, but a supernatural infusion and implantation. "I will put my fear in their hearts" (Jer. 32:40). To fear man is natural; to fear God is wholly supernatural. (2) This fear puts the soul under the awe of God's eye. "My heart standeth in awe of thy word" (Ps. 119:161b). It is the reproach of people's servants to be eye-servants, but it is the praise and honor of God's servants to be so. (3) This fear inclines us to do what pleases God. Hence, fearing God and working righteousness are related (Acts 10:35). If we fear God, we dare not ignore what He commands. If His fear is exalted in our hearts, it will enable us to obey Him in duties accompanied with deep self-denial. "Now I know that thou fearest God, seeing thou hast not withheld thy son, thine only son from me" (Gen. 22:12b). (4) This fear engages and, to some degree, enables the soul to shun and avoid whatever displeases God. Job refused to touch what God had forbidden. Therefore, God honored him with this excellent description: he was "one that feared God, and eschewed evil" (Job 1:1b).

Thus you have the types of fear.

CHAPTER 3

Uses of Fear

Having briefly viewed the various types of fear that are found among us, our next task is to consider their uses in the government of this world. In one way or another, they are subservient to God's wise and holy purposes.

The Use of Natural Fear

We begin with natural fear. It is absolutely necessary for our civil governance. By consequence, it is necessary for the world's peace, order, and comfort. This passion acts like a bridle, curbing our corrupt inclinations. If God had not planted it in us, our nature's corruptions would make us incapable of any moral restraint from the most heinous and barbarous crimes. If fear did not clasp its chains and shackles upon our wild and boisterous lusts, we would suppress all milder motives and break loose from all bands of restraint; the world would be filled with disorder, tumult, theft, murder, and all manner of uncleanness and unrighteousness. People would become like the fish of the sea, as the prophet complains

(Hab. 1:14); the greater would swallow up a multitude
of the smaller. Decency would disappear from the world.
No one would be safe; the capacity and opportunity to
do mischief would result in the break-up of all societies.

This observation is true: Whoever fears not the
loss of his own life will master another person's life. It
is the law and the accompanying fear of punishment
that keeps the world in order. People are afraid to do
evil because they are afraid to suffer for it. They see
that the law has inseparably linked moral and punish-
able evils together. If they presume to commit the one,
they must necessarily suffer the other. This keeps them
in some order and decorum. Without law, there would
be no order or security. If laws had no penalties annexed
to them, they would have no more power to restrain our
corruptions than the new ropes had to bind Samson
(Judg. 16:11). And yet, even if the severest penalties are
annexed to laws, they are meaningless without natural
fear. It is a tender, sensible passion, deeply affected by
threats. It brings people under moral government and
restraint. "For rulers are not a terror to good works, but
to the evil.... But if thou do that which is evil, be afraid;
for he beareth not the sword in vain" (Rom. 13:3–4a).
By this means, fear restrains and prevents a world of evil.

Upon their king's death, it was the Persians' cus-
tom (I am not saying it was laudable) to grant everyone
liberty for five days to do whatever they wanted. The
unbridled lust was so great that it made the people long

and pray for the installment of their next king. In this way it endeared government to them. Blessed be God for law and government, for using them to curb people's raging lusts, and thereby procuring rest and comfort for us in the world!

The Use of Sinful Fear

This kind of fear is formally evil and sinful in its own nature. It is also the fruit of sin and the offspring of sinful nature. Yet, God knows how to overrule it in His providential government of the world to His own wise and holy purposes.

First, God uses sinful fear as a scourge to punish His enemies. If people will not fear God, then they will fear one another. He will make them a terror to themselves. God's deliverance of a person into the hands of his own fear is a dreadful punishment indeed. There is scarcely a greater torment in the world than for a person to be his own tormentor and for his mind to be an engine of torture to his body. In 2 Kings 17:25, we read that God sent lions among the people. But that is not as bad as God letting loose our own fears upon us. No lion is as cruel as this passion. David esteemed it a great blessing when God delivered him from all his fears (Ps. 34:4). God's threats against the disobedient and rebellious are dreadful: "And among these nations shalt thou find no ease, neither shall the sole of thy foot have rest: but the LORD shall give thee there a trembling heart, and failing of eyes, and sorrow of mind: and thy life shall hang in doubt before thee; and thou shalt fear day and night, and shalt have none assurance of thy life: in the morning thou shalt say, Would God it were even! and at even thou shalt say, Would God it were morning! for the fear of thine heart wherewith thou shalt fear, and for the sight of thine eyes which thou shalt see" (Deut. 28:65–67). When fear seizes the heart, we see death's color displayed in the face. What a dismal life for those who have neither peace by day nor rest by night, but wearisome days and nights! The days of such people are tiresome. They wish for the night, hoping it will give them a little rest. But their fear goes to bed with them. Their hearts pant in terror. They cry, "Oh that it were day again!"

Second, God uses sinful fear to punish His enemies in hell. This terrible affliction accounts for a great part of their torment. Divines make this threefold distinction of torments in hell. (1) God punishes the wicked through the remembrance of things past. The mercies and means, which they once experienced, are irrecoverably lost. (2) God punishes the wicked through the sense of things present. God's wrath encompasses their souls and bodies. (3) God punishes the wicked through the fear of things future. This is not the least part of their misery. Oh, fearful expectation of fiery indignation— more and more of God's wrath still approaching, as the waves of the sea, thrusting forward one upon another! That is what makes the devils tremble (James 2:19).

The word in this verse signifies a noise like the roar of the sea—the roar of the waves as they break against the rocks. Fear, which continually strikes like a whip, causes this trembling.

Third, God uses sinful or slavish fear to scatter wicked people, especially when they align themselves against His people. This fear puts them to flight when no other visible power can do it. God casts out the heathen before His people Israel (Ps. 78:55). How did God subdue those mighty nations? He did not do it through the strength of Israel's multitudes, but through the nations' fear: "And I sent the hornet before you, which drave them out from before you" (Josh. 24:12a). These hornets were the fears and terrors of their own guilty minds which buzzed and swarmed in their hearts. They stung them to the heart worse than the Israelites' swords. Theodoret, bishop of Cyrrhus, in Syria, relates the story of Sapores, king of Persia, who had besieged Christians in the city of Nisibis. He put them to such straits that little hope of safety remained. But in the depth of their distress, God sent an army of hornets and gnats among their enemies. They entered into the elephants' ears and trunks, and the horses' nostrils. This so enraged them that they broke their harnesses, cast their riders, and scattered. By this providence, the Christians escaped. These hornets were terrible, but fear (which, figuratively speaking, is a hornet) is ten thousand times worse. It sinks the strongest person's heart. It makes the proud and haughty, who act like gods, to realize that they are mere mortals. "Put them in fear, O LORD: that the nations may know themselves to be but men" (Ps. 9:20). One fright will awaken them from a thousand fond conceits and idle dreams.

The Use of Religious Fear

If God can cause fruit to grow upon such a bramble as sinful fear, then what can He do with religious fear—a choice root planted by His Spirit? The uses and benefits are innumerable and inestimable, but I will only mention three.

First, God uses it to excite and confirm His people in the way of their duty. "Fear God, and keep his commandments" (Eccl. 12:13). Religious fear is the keeper of both tables of the law because it influences the duties of both tables. It makes us give due respect to all of God's commands. It is powerful enough to confirm us in, and excite us to, our duties. "I will put my fear in their hearts, that they shall not depart from me" (Jer. 32:40b). The person who sows does not regard the wind, but persists in his work—whatever the weather. Likewise, the person who fears God persists in the way of his duty. That provides a great advantage in times of fear and distraction. Slavish fear sets a person upon the devil's ground but religious fear sets him upon God's ground. How important is the choice of our ground, when we are about to suffer a great affliction!

Second, God uses this fear to preserve our conscience's peace and purity. It does so by preventing grief and guilt. "And by the fear of the LORD men depart from evil" (Prov. 16:6b). It preserved Joseph (Gen. 39:9) and Nehemiah (Neh. 5:15). This benefit is invaluable, especially in a day of outward calamity and distress. Our consciences' peace is directly proportionate to the degree to which the fear of God prevails in our hearts. The same is true of our strength and comfort in the evil day, and of our courage and confidence in the face of danger.

Third, God uses this fear to make us prepare for future distress. As a result, we are not surprised when it comes upon us. Thus, Noah "moved with fear, prepared an ark" (Heb. 11:7). His fear was the instrument of his and his family's salvation. Some men owe their death to their fear, but good men (in a sense) owe their lives to their fear. Sinful fear has slain some while godly fear has saved others. "A wise man feareth, and departeth from evil: but the fool rageth, and is confident" (Prov. 14:16). A wise man's fear sounds a timely alarm, before the enemy falls upon him. By this means, he has time to get into his secure chamber before the storm arrives. But the fool "rageth, and is confident." He never fears until he begins to feel. More often than not he is past all hope before he begins to experience any fear.

These are some of the uses God makes of the different types of fear.

CHAPTER 4

Causes of Sinful Fear

Having demonstrated the types and uses of fear, we will next consider the causes of sinful fear.

Cause 1: Ignorance

The sinful fear of most good people arises from their ignorance—the darkness of their minds. All darkness inclines to fear, but none like intellectual darkness. Among Solomon's guards, "every man hath his sword upon his thigh because of fear in the night" (Song 3:8b). The night is a frightful time. In the dark, every bush is a bear. We smile at day-break when we see what silly things scared us during the night. So it is here; if our judgment is properly instructed, our hearts will be at peace. There is a five-fold ignorance from which our fear arises.

First, we are ignorant of God. We do not know (or, at least, we do not fully consider) His almighty power, vigilant care, unspotted faithfulness, and how these are engaged by covenant for His people. Such ignorance lies at the root of the Israelites' fear: "My way is hid from the

LORD, and my judgment is passed over from my God"
(Isa. 40:27b). These words express their suspicion that
God has abandoned them. Their suspicion stems from
their misunderstanding of His providence. If we thoroughly understand and believe what power is in God's
hand to defend us, what tenderness is in His heart to
help us, and what faithfulness is in His promises, our
hearts will be calm—our courage will grow stronger
and our fear will grow weaker.

Second, we are ignorant of others. We fear people
because we do not know them. If we were to understand
them better, we would fear them less. We overvalue
them; therefore, we fear them. Apparently, the artist
often paints the lion fiercer than he is. I am sure our
imagination paints people more dreadful than they are.
If wicked people, especially multitudes, align themselves
against us, our hearts fail and we perceive inevitable
ruin. "The floods of ungodly men made me afraid"
(2 Sam. 22:5b). David means he feared those whom he
thought would sweep him away as a mighty torrent of
water sweeps away a feather. We fail to consider that
people have no power over us except what God gives
them from above. God usually clasps on the bands of
restraint when their hearts are fully set to do us mischief. If we were to consider them as they are in God's
hand, we would not tremble at them.

Third, we are ignorant of ourselves. Our failure to
appreciate our relation to God creates slavish fear in our

hearts (Isa. 51:12). If we were to understand how dear
we are to God, our relation to Him, our value in His
eyes, and how He protects us by His faithful promises
and gracious presence, we would not tremble at every
appearance of danger. God reckoned it enough to cure
Abraham's sinful fear when He told him how He stood
ready for his defense: "Fear not, Abram, I am thy shield"
(Gen. 15:1). In times of fear and danger, noble Nehemiah valued himself according to his interest in God.
The conspiracy against him was strong. The danger was
extraordinary. Some people advised him to flee to the
temple and barricade himself against the enemy. But
Nehemiah understood himself better: "Should such
a man as I flee? and who is there, that, being as I am,
would go into the temple to save his life? I will not go
in" (Neh. 6:11). Nehemiah was called of God. He knew
God's promises. He had manifest and manifold experiences of God's goodness. Should such a man flee? Other
people, who have no such encouragements, might flee,
but not Nehemiah. In his bloody times, Tertullian used
a similar argument to calm the Christians' fears: "Are
you afraid of a man, Christian, when devils are afraid
of you? The world ought to fear you, seeing as you will
judge it." If only we could, without pride and vanity,
value ourselves according to our Christian dignities and
privileges! If ever it is necessary to count them, it is in
times of fear and danger, when the heart is so prone to
dejection and sinking fears.

Fourth, we are ignorant of our circumstances. We mistake our dangers and troubles; hence, we fear them. In particular, we are ignorant of the comforts in them and the escapes from them. There is a vast difference between trouble's outward appearance and inward reality. From a distance, it is a lion; but when we open it, we discover honey in its belly (Judg. 14:8). Paul and Silas experienced this in prison and it enabled them to sing at midnight (Acts 16:25). Many others have done the same. Not only are we ignorant of the comforts that are found in our troubles, but we are ignorant of the doors of escape. "And unto God the Lord belong the issues from death" (Ps. 68:20b). "The LORD knoweth how to deliver the godly out of temptation" (2 Peter 2:9a). "[God] will with the temptation also make a way to escape, that ye may be able to bear it" (1 Cor. 10:13b). The poor captive exiles expected to die; therefore, they made their graves in the land of their captivity. They could only think of the usual methods of deliverance: power or payment. They had neither. They never dreamed of God's immediate influences upon the king's heart to make him release them—contrary to all rules of state policy (Isa. 45:12–13).

Fifth, we are ignorant of the covenant of grace. If we were better acquainted with the nature, extent, and stability of this covenant, our hearts would be free from these tormenting passions. This covenant is a universal remedy against all our fears—on spiritual or temporal accounts. We will return to this later.

Cause 2: Guilt

Another cause and fountain of sinful fear is a guilty conscience. A servant of sin is necessarily a slave of fear. Those who commit evil must expect evil. As soon as Adam defiled and wounded his conscience with guilt, he trembled and hid himself. It is the same way with his children. God calls to Adam, not with threats, but with gentle words—not in a storm, but in the cool of the day. Even so, it terrifies Adam because his conscience condemns him (Gen. 3:8). Seneca, a Roman philosopher, observes that a guilty conscience acts as a terrible torment to the sinner, perpetually lashing him with fears. He does not know where to find security. He dares not trust in any promises of protection. He doubts. He is jealous of everything. He has "a dreadful sound...in his ears" (Job 15:21), meaning he suffers the effects of real and imaginary dangers. His troubled imagination scares him, even when there is no real danger. "The wicked flee when no man pursueth: but the righteous are bold as a lion" (Prov. 28:1). Sheep are frightened by the clattering of their own feet; likewise, the guilty sinner is frightened by the noise of his own conscience. It sounds misery, wrath, and hell in his ears. We may say of wicked people, in their fear, as Tacitus (a Roman senator and historian) does of tyrants, "If it were possible to open their minds and consciences, we would find many terrible stripes and wounds."

It is said, "The sinners in Zion are afraid" (Isa. 33:14a). Trembling takes hold of the hypocrite. Fear and trembling arise out of guilt as naturally as sparks fly out of the furnace. History furnishes us with many sad examples. Charles IX, king of France, after his bloody and barbarous massacre of the Protestants, could neither sleep nor wake without music to divert his thoughts. Richard III, king of England, after the murder of his two innocent nephews, saw shapes like devils pulling at him in his sleep. The opposite of this wounded and trembling conscience is the spirit of a sound mind: "For God hath not given us the spirit of fear; but of power, and of love, and of a sound mind" (2 Tim. 1:7). A sound mind is the same thing as a pure and peaceable conscience—a conscience not wounded with guilt. Such a mind is opposed to the spirit of fear. It makes a person as bold as a lion.

An evil and guilty conscience produces fears and terrors in three ways. (1) It aggravates small matters, blowing them up to the height of the most fatal and destructive evils. Cain cries, "Every one that findeth me shall slay me" (Gen. 4:14b). Every child became a giant in his sight and everyone he met became a threat. A guilty conscience gives a person a view of his enemy through a magnifying glass. (2) It interprets all doubtful cases in the worst possible sense. (3) It creates fears and terrors out of nothing. In arithmetic, many zeros make zero. The rules of fear, however, are not like that. It can make something out of nothing—many and great things out of nothing at all. "There were they in great fear where no fear was" (Ps. 53:5a). Here is a great fear created out of nothing. When traced back to its cause, it is discovered that this fear is a pure product of the imagination. It has no other foundation than a guilty conscience. Pashur was a wicked man. He was a terror to himself—afraid of his own shadow (Jer. 20:3–4). Truly, this is a great plague and misery. He who is a terror to himself can no more flee from terrors than from himself. Oh, the efficacy of conscience! How it arrests the strongest sinners and makes them tremble when there is no visible, external cause of fear! No guilty man is absolved, even when he himself acts the part of judge.

Some people object, "There are many good and pardoned people, who are frightened by their imaginations." It is true, for there is a twofold fountain of fear—one in the body (constitution) and one in the soul (conscience). It is the affliction and unhappiness of many pardoned and gracious souls to be united to diseased bodies that afflict them from within. They wound them by their own diseases and infections. These wounds cannot be cured and prevented by reason or religion any more than bodily disease can be cured by such things. This is a sore affliction for many good people, whose consciences are sprinkled with Christ's blood. God sees fit to burden them with such affliction for their humiliation and the prevention of greater evil.

Other people object, "There are many bold and daring sinners, who (despite their guilty conscience) look danger in the face without trembling. They look death—the king of terrors—in the face with less fear than better men." It is true; however, the reason for it is God's spiritual judgment upon their hearts and consciences, whereby they are hardened and seared with a hot iron (1 Tim. 4:2). As a result, the conscience no longer functions as it ought. At present, it cannot put forth its power and activity when it might be useful to their salvation. But it will, in the future, when their case will be without remedy.

Cause 3: Unbelief

A guilty conscience is a source of fears, but the sin of unbelief is the real and proper cause of most distracting and afflicting fears. To the extent that our souls are empty of faith, they are filled with fear. We read of people who have died by no other cause than their fear. But we never read of anyone, once brought to life by faith, dying because of fear. If people were to dig to the root of their fears, they would find unbelief. "Why are ye fearful, O ye of little faith?" (Matt. 8:26). The weaker the faith, the greater the fear; unbelief generates fear and fear strengthens unbelief. In nature, there is an observable, circular generation: vapors produce showers and showers produce vapors. It is the same way in moral things. All the skill in the world cannot cure us of the disease of fear. God must first cure us of our unbelief. Christ took the right method to rid His disciples of their fear when He rebuked them for their unbelief. The remnant of this sin in God's people is the fountain of their fears. As for how unbelief generates fear, consider the following points.

First, unbelief weakens the assenting act of faith. In so doing, it severs the soul from its principal relief against danger and trouble. It is the office of faith to impress upon the soul the invisible things of the world to come, thereby encouraging it against the fears and dangers of the present world. "By faith [Moses] forsook Egypt, not fearing the wrath of the king: for he endured, as seeing him who is invisible" (Heb. 11:27). If this assenting act of faith is weakened in the soul, if the invisible seems to be uncertain and the visible seems to be the only reality, then it is no wonder that we are frightened when visible and sensible comforts are threatened—as they often are in this changing world. The person who is not thoroughly persuaded that he stands upon firm ground will be afraid to stand his ground. It is no surprise that those who tremble think they feel the ground shake beneath them.

Second, unbelief severs the soul from its refuge in the divine promises. In so doing, it leaves the soul in the hand of fears and terrors. In evil times, a Christian is fortified and emboldened by his dependence upon God for protection. "I flee unto thee to hide me" (Ps. 143:9b). The removal of this refuge (which only unbelief can do) deprives the soul of all the help and support that God's promises supply. As a result, it fills the heart with fear and anxiety.

Third, unbelief makes people careless and negligent in preparing for trouble. As a result, they are taken by surprise. The more surprising evil is, the more frightening it is. Noah was not as frightened as the rest of the world when the flood waters began to swell above the hills and mountains. There was no reason for him to be afraid, since he had foreseen it by faith. "By faith Noah, being warned of God of things not seen as yet, moved with fear, prepared an ark" (Heb. 11:7a). Augustine relates a memorable story of Paulinas, bishop of Nola, who was rich in both goods and graces. He had much of the world in his hands, but little of it in his heart. When the Goths, a barbarous people, sacked his city, they seized the spoils. Those who trusted in their treasure were ruined. The Goths afflicted them with torture in order to make them tell where they had hidden their wealth. This good bishop also fell into their hands. He lost everything, yet he remained unmoved at the loss. He prayed, "Lord, let me not be troubled for my gold and silver. Thou knowest it is not my treasure—that which I have laid up in heaven according to Thy command. Thou hast warned of this judgment before it came and I prepared for it. Thou knowest, Lord, where my interest lies." In the same way, when the jailor's wife came running into John Bradford's chamber with news

that would have terrified most men—"Oh, Mr. Bradford! I bring you heavy tidings. Tomorrow, you will
be burned"—he declared, "Lord, I thank Thee. I have
waited for this for a long time. It is not terrible to me.
God, make me worthy of such a mercy." Oh, the benefit
of preparing for suffering!

Fourth, unbelief leaves our dearest interests and
concerns in our own hands. It commits nothing to God.
Consequently, it fills the heart with distracting fears
when imminent danger threatens us. If this is your case,
you will be surrounded with terror whenever you are
surrounded with danger and trouble. Believers have this
advantage: they have committed by faith all that is precious and valuable to them into God's hands. They have
committed the keeping of their souls (1 Peter 4:19) and
all their eternal concerns (2 Tim. 1:14) to Him. Because
these things are in safe hands, they are not distracted
with fears about matters of less value. They entrust these
to God and enjoy the peace and quietness of a resigned
soul (Prov. 16:3). But as for you, you keep your life, liberty, and soul (which is infinitely greater than these other
things) in your own hands in the day of trouble. You do
not know what to do with them or how to dispose of
them. Oh, these are the dreadful frights in which unbelief leaves people! It is a fountain of fears and distractions.
Indeed, it cannot but distract and bewilder carnal people,
in whom it reigns in full strength. Sad experience shows
us what fear (the remains and relics of unbelief) produces

in the best people, who are not fully free from it. If the relics of unbelief can darken and cloud their evidences, if it can draw such sad and frightful conclusions in their hearts (despite all the contrary experience of their lives), what unrelieved terrors must it produce in those who are under its full strength and dominion!

Cause 4: Confusion

The administration of God's providence in this world provokes many of our fears. "All things come alike to all: there is one event to the righteous, and to the wicked; to the good and to the clean, and to the unclean; to him that sacrificeth, and to him that sacrificeth not" (Eccl. 9:2). "Behold, I am against thee, and will draw forth my sword out of his sheath, and will cut off from thee the righteous and the wicked" (Ezek. 21:3b). The sword makes no difference where God has made a difference by grace. It does not distinguish between faces or hearts. It is as soon plunged into the hearts of the best as the worst people. We read that the fire of God's indignation devours the green tree and dry tree (Ezek. 20:47), that the baskets of "good figs" (emblems of the best people) are carried into Babylon along with the bad (Jer. 24:5), that the flesh of God's saints is given as meat to the fowls of the air and the beasts of the field (Ps. 79:2), and that the wicked devour the righteous (Hab. 1:13). We observe such things in Scripture and our observations are confirmed in history. We reflect upon the unspeakable miseries of those precious servants of Christ (the Albigenses and Waldenses)—how they fell as prey to cruel adversaries, despite the convincing holiness of their lives and their fervent cries and appeals to God. We reflect upon the Reformed Protestant interest in France, which was cut off with such barbarous inhumanity to the extent that the streets and canals of Paris were filled with precious blood. We reflect upon the horrid and unparalleled torture of God's servants during the cruel massacre in Ireland—a history too tragic for a tender-hearted reader. We reflect upon those eminent ministers and Christians in our own land who were sent to heaven in a fiery chariot in Queen Mary's dreadful days. When we read and consider such things, our fear is stirred. When the feet of those who carried out God's dear servants in bloody sheets to their graves stand at the door to carry us out (if providence grants them permission to do so), our fear is heightened. Rather than thinking on things that fortify faith and heighten courage, we think on these things, thereby increasing our fear. There are four things in particular that tend to occupy our thoughts.

First, we think that these same people who committed such atrocities are still found today. Their rage and malice are as fierce and cruel as ever. "But as then he that was born after the flesh persecuted him that was born after the Spirit, even so it is now" (Gal. 4:29). As it was then, so it is still. The old enmity is found in wicked people from generation to generation. Cain's club (stained with Abel's blood) is still carried in the world. It is a deep-rooted hatred, which runs in blood. It will run as long as there are wicked people to propagate it and a devil to exasperate it.

Second, we think that nothing hinders the execution of their wicked purposes except the restraints of providence. If God were to loose the chain and permit them to act according to the rage and malice in their hearts, they would not show us any pity (Ps. 124:1–6). We live among lions—those who are set on fire by hell (Ps. 57:4). The only reason for our safety is this: the Keeper of the lions is also the Shepherd of the sheep.

Third, we think that God, on many occasions, has released these lions upon His people. He has allowed them to tear His lambs in pieces and suck the blood of His saints. However much He loves His people, He has often delivered them into the hands of their enemies. He has allowed their enemies to perpetrate the greatest cruelties upon them. The best people have suffered the worst things. History delivers to us the most tragic details of their barbarous treatment.

Fourth, we think that we fall far short in holiness, innocence, and spiritual maturity in comparison to those excellent saints who suffered these things; therefore, we have no ground to expect more favor from providence. We know that they had the same Scripture promises as we have. Moreover, we know that there are greater sins in us than in them; therefore, we have no reason to imagine that we are exempt. If we do not think these evils will come in our day, we must remember that many of them thought the same thing. "The kings of the earth, and all the inhabitants of the world, would not have believed that the adversary and the enemy should have entered into the gates of Jerusalem" (Lam. 4:12).

The revolving of these and other considerations in our thoughts, and the mixing of our own unbelief with them, creates a world of fear—even in good people. This continues until we resign everything to God, setting our faith upon His promises, which assure us of His sanctification of our troubles (Rom. 8:28), His presence with us in our troubles (Ps. 92:15), His moderation of our troubles to a degree we can endure (Isa. 26:8), and His final deliverance of us from our troubles (Rev. 7:17). In this way, we rescue our hearts from our fear and compose them to a quiet and sweet satisfaction in the wise and holy pleasure of our God.

Cause 5: Immoderation

Our immoderate love of life and its comforts and conveniences is another cause of sinful fear in times of danger. If we loved our lives less, we would fear and tremble less. It is said of those renowned saints: "And they overcame him by the blood of the Lamb, and by the word of their testimony; and they loved not their lives unto the death" (Rev. 12:11). They overcame their enemies' fury from without and their sinful fears from within. They achieved this victory through death to the inordinate and immoderate love of life. Certainly, their fear would have overcome them if they had not first overcome their love of life. It is not, therefore, without great reason that our Lord commands His disciples to hate their own lives (Luke 14:26)—not absolutely, but in comparison to their love for Him. We are to esteem our lives as poor, lowly things in comparison to our love for Him. He knew what suffering would come upon them. If the immoderate love of life were not overcome and mortified, it would make them bend under such temptations.

That is what freed Paul from slavish fear and made him so undaunted. Although he suffered hard things, he had less fear than his friends, who only sympathized with him in his suffering. He spoke like a spectator rather than a sufferer, declaring, "None of these things move me" (Acts 20:24a). How did he obtain such courage and constancy of mind in the midst of such deep and dreadful suffering? His suffering was enough to move the bravest person in the world and to remove the resolution of anyone who did not love Christ more than life. But in comparison to Jesus Christ, life was a trifle to Paul. He tells us: "Neither count I my life dear unto myself" (Acts 20:24). In other words, "It is a commodity of little value in my eyes—not worth saving on such sinful terms." Oh, how many have parted with Christ, peace, and eternal life for fear of losing what Paul so little regarded! If we bring our thoughts nearer the matter, we will find that this is a fountain of fear in times of danger. From this excessive love of life, we are racked and tortured with ten thousand terrors. Why?

First, life is the natural man's greatest and closest interest in this world. All other interests are wrapped up in it. "Skin for skin, yea, all that a man hath will he give for his life" (Job 2:4). It is true, even though it came from the mouth of the father of lies. Afflictions never touch the quick until they touch the life. Liberty, estates, and other accommodations in this world receive their value and estimation from life. If life is cut off, these things perish and are of no account. "Behold, I am at the point to die: and what profit shall this birthright do to me?" (Gen. 25:32).

Second, since life is the natural man's dearest interest, richest treasure, and most beloved thing on earth, whatever endangers life must be the greatest evil. On this account, death becomes terrible to people. Job calls it "the king of terrors" (Job 18:14b). It is so terrible that fear of it has driven some people into its hands. For example, in times of outbreak the excessive fear of the plague has induced death.

Third, although death is terrible in its mildest form, it is most terrible in a violent and bloody form—at the hands of cruel and merciless people. This is "the king of terrors" indeed, in its most ghastly and frightful form, in its scarlet robes. In a violent death, all the barbarous cruelties that our enemies can invent (or their malice can inflict) are mingled together. In a violent death, many deaths are converted into one. Oftentimes, it approaches people with such slow and deliberate paces that they feel its every step. "Let him so die," said the tyrant, "that he may feel himself to die." This is exceedingly frightful, especially to those who are of soft and tender natures. They are pierced with the terror of death, unless the Lord arms them against it with the assurance of a better life and sweetens their bitter apprehensions by foretastes of it. It is enough to horrify sanctified nature and make a gracious heart sink, unless divine strength and comfort uphold it. When enemies who are accustomed to this bloody work design to break upon us and inflict such cruelty upon us, our fear and terror arise.

Cause 6: Satan

Many of our sinful fears flow from Satan's influences upon our imaginations. It is said that Satan raises winds and storms, both by sea and land. I have never doubted that the prince of the power of the air, by God's permission, can put the world into great frights and disturbances by such tempests (Job 1:19). He can raise the loftiest winds, pour down roaring showers, rattle in the air with fearful claps of thunder, and scare the lower world with terrible flashes of lightning. I do not doubt that he has, by God's permission, a great deal of influence upon people's imaginations and passions. He can raise far more terrible storms and tempests within than we ever felt without. He can approach our imaginations, disturbing them with frightful ideas. Satan not only works upon people through their external senses. By reason of his spiritual and angelical nature, he has immediate access to their internal senses. This appears in diabolical dreams.

By working on the imagination, he influences its passions and puts it under dreadful apprehensions and distractions. Now, if Satan can provoke and exasperate the fury and rage of wicked men (as is evident he can) and can go to the storehouses of thunder, lightning, and storms, then with what inward storms of fear can he shake our hearts! If God gives him permission, he is ready to do it, seeing as it is so conducible to his design. By putting men into such frights, he weakens their hands in duty. That is how he tempted Nehemiah (Neh. 6:13). If he prevails, he drives them into temptation's snare as the fishermen and fowlers trap birds and fish in their nets, having flushed them out of the woods.

Thus you have some idea of the principal causes of sinful fear.

CHAPTER 5

Effects of Sinful Fear

Having viewed in the former chapters the types and causes of fear, and having examined what lies at the root of slavish fear, what breeds and feeds it, we now turn to the deplorable effects of such fear. Our consideration of its fruit will motivate us to apply ourselves most earnestly to the directions that are found later in this book.

Effect 1: Distraction

The first effect of this sinful passion is distraction of mind in duty. Both Cicero (a Roman philosopher) and Quintilian (a Roman rhetorician) maintain that the Latin word *tumultus* (tumult) consists of *timor* (fear) and *multus* (much). Much fear creates great tumult in the soul. It puts everything into hurries and distractions to such an extent that we cannot perform any service for God with profit or comfort. The following request is a much needed mercy: "That we, being delivered out of the hands of our enemies, might serve him without fear" (Luke 1:74b). It is impossible to serve God without distractions until we can serve Him without the slavish fear of enemies. The reverential fear of God is the greatest spur to duty and the best help in it. But the distracting fear of enemies will divert us from our duty, thereby destroying its comfort and benefit. The devil's hindrance of comfortable fellowship with God is a deadly snare.

It is remarkable that when the apostle advises the Corinthians about marriage in times of persecution, he commends a single life. He does so for this reason: that they might "attend upon the Lord without distraction" (1 Cor. 7:35b). He knows what straits, cares, and fears unavoidably distract those who are encumbered with families and relations in such times. People should be asking, "What should I do to resolve my fears and doubts concerning my interest in Christ? How should I behave in suffering so as to credit religion, and not become a scandal and stumbling-block to others?" Instead, their thoughts are occupied with other cares and fears: "What will become of my wife and little ones? What will I do to secure them from danger?"

I do not doubt that it is one of the devil's great designs to keep us in continual fear and alarm, and to puzzle our heads and hearts with a thousand difficulties, which will probably never come upon us (even if they do, they will never prove as fatal as we imagine). He does this to unfit us for present duties and to destroy our comfort in them. If he can distract our thoughts through fears and terrors, he gains three advantages to our unspeakable loss.

First, he severs us from the freedom and sweetness of communion with God in duties. The best duties become an empty shell when this worm eats away at them. Prayer, as John of Damascus expresses it, is the ascension of the mind or soul to God. But distraction clips its wings. Whoever lacks possession of his thoughts never offers up his soul to God. The life of communion with God in prayer consists in the harmony that is between our hearts and words, and both with God's will. Distraction spoils this harmony.

Second, Satan severs the soul from the support and relief it should draw from God's promises. When the Israelites were in bondage, their minds were distracted with fears and sorrows. They did not regard Moses' supporting promises of deliverance (Ex. 6:6). David received a particular promise of the kingdom from God's mouth. It included his deliverance from Saul's hand—all his attempts to destroy him. Even so, when he faced imminent hazards, he was afraid. That fear undermined the support he should have derived from the promise to such an extent that he declared: "I shall now perish one day by the hand of Saul" (1 Sam. 27:1). He also declared, "All men are liars" (Ps. 116:11). That included Samuel, who had assured David of the kingdom. This is always the nature of fear (as I have already demonstrated): it makes people distrust the best security when they are in imminent peril. What a mischief is this—to make us suspicious of those promises that are our chief relief and support in times of trouble! Our fears will render us unfit for prayer. They will also shake the credit of the promises. The damage to us is so great that it would be better to lose our two eyes than to lose such advantages in trouble.

Third, Satan severs us from the comfort that is found in our past experiences and the relief that God's faithfulness and goodness imparted in former straits and dangers. Fear clouds them all (Isa. 51:12–13). We give so much attention to people and dangers that we forget God—even the God who preserved us when the enemy was ready to devour us. Our distracting fears cut us off from all these sweet reliefs when we need them most.

Effect 2: Deception

Deception is also the fruit of slavish fear. Distraction is bad enough, but deceit is even worse. Yet, as bad as it is, fear drives good people into this snare. It makes an upright soul warp and bend from those rules of integrity which should be inseparable from a Christian. God says to Israel, "And of whom hast thou been afraid or feared, that thou hast lied, and hast not remembered me, nor laid it to thy heart?" (Isa. 57:11a). God blames fear for their falsehood. It was against the resolution of their hearts to waver. Who has scared you into this evil?

Abraham's fear made him waver at the reproach of his religion (Gen. 20: 2, 11). It was an odd sight to see a heathen reprove great Abraham. Fear drew his son, Isaac, into the same snare (Gen. 26:7). Despite Christ's promise, fear caused Peter to say: "I do not know the man" (Matt. 26:72b). Abraham should have remembered what the Lord had said to him: "Fear not, Abram, I am thy shield" (Gen. 15:1). If he had, he would have escaped both the sin and the shame into which he fell. Yet, fear was even able to foil this great believer.

Certainly this is a great evil, a complicated mischief. (1) It dishonors God. Through these falls and scandals, religion is made vile and contemptible in the world's eyes. It brings much reproach upon God and His promises, as if His Word were insufficient security in times of trouble, as if it were safer to sin than to trust His promises. (2) It weakens other believers. It is a sore discouragement in times of trial to see our brothers faint for fear—to see them ashamed to hold to their own principles. Satan and wicked people always use it to this purpose. (3) It wounds the conscience. Such flaws in integrity will keep us awake at night. Oh, the mischief caused by a faint and fearful spirit!

Effect 3: Vulnerability

Slavish fear strengthens temptation in times of danger and makes it very prevalent and influential. "The fear of man bringeth a snare" (Prov. 29:25a). Satan spreads the net, but we are not within its reach until our own fear drives us into it. The soul's recoiling from imminent danger might cause a true Christian's pulse to falter—no matter how regular it beats at other times. It causes great trepidation and timidity in people who are sincere and upright. It brings the snare over their souls. Aaron was a good man and he knew idolatry was a great sin. Yet, fear prevailed upon him to such an extent that he gave way to that great evil. "Thou knowest the people, that they are set on mischief" (Ex. 32:22b). In other words, "Lord, I had no choice. The people were violently and passionately set upon it. If I had resisted them, it would have cost me dearly."

Fear prevailed upon Origen to yield in offering incense to idols. Fear made David play the fool and act so dishonorably (1 Sam. 21:12–15). Fear is Satan's snare. It has caught as many souls as any other snare. It would be easy to give many sad examples, but it would make this chapter too long. Instead, I will give a few particulars concerning this snare's danger.

First, fear drives people out of their proper station, out of their place and duty into Satan's ground. The subtle enemy of our salvation knows that we are out of gunshot range when we abide with God in the way of our duty. The Lord is with us while we are with Him. Satan cannot attempt to ruin us while we are under the wings of God's protection. To do anything to us, he must first force us out from under those wings. Nothing does this more effectively than fear. When we move from that shelter, we are like birds wandering from their nests (Prov. 27:8).

Second, fear is usually the first passion to seek peace with the enemy. It approaches the tempter about terms of surrender. As the French proverb says, "The castle that parleys is half won." Fear consults with flesh and blood, while faith engages with God to supply strength to endure the siege. We have a sad instance of this in Mr. Bacon's account of Francis Spira—a lawyer, who renounced his commitment to Luther's cause. His fears caused him to parley with the tempter.

> While Spira tossed upon the restless waves of doubt, without guide to trust or haven to flee for help, God's Spirit suddenly assisted him. He felt calm and began to converse with himself in this manner: "Why do you wander in uncertainty? Unhappy man! Cast away fear, put on your shield of faith! Where are your courage, goodness, and constancy? Remember that Christ's glory lies at the stake! Suffer, therefore, without fear! He will defend you. He will tell you how to answer. He can beat back all danger, bring you out of prison, and raise you from the dead. Consider Peter in the dungeon and the martyrs in the fire." Spira was quiet and resolved to follow those weighty reasons. However, thinking it wise to examine all things, he consulted flesh and blood. As a result, the battle resumed. Flesh spoke as follow: "Be well advised. Consider reasons on both sides; then judge. How can you overvalue your own sufficiency? You neither regard the examples of your forefathers, nor the judgment of the whole church. Do you not consider what misery this rashness will cause you? You will lose all your substance obtained with so

much care and travail. You will undergo the most exquisite torments that malice can devise. You will be viewed as a heretic. On top of everything, you will die shamefully. What do you think of the stinking dungeon, the bloody axe, and the burning wood? Are they delightful?" Through fear, Spira parleyed with the tempter, consulted with flesh and blood, and at last fainted and yielded.

Third, fear makes people impatient while waiting for God's time and method of deliverance. It discourages the soul and drives it into the next temptation's snare. "The captive exile hasteneth that he may be loosed, and that he should not die in the pit" (Isa. 51:14). According to fear, any means of escape is better than lying in a pit. When fear influences the soul, it becomes easy prey to the next temptation.

Effect 4: Cowardice

Fear naturally produces cowardice in people—a poor, low spirit that faints and yields upon every slight assault. Wherever it prevails, it extinguishes Christian courage and strength. In the Scriptures, it is frequently joined with discouragement. "Fear not, neither be discouraged" (Deut. 1:21b). "Let not your hearts faint, fear not, and do not tremble, neither be ye terrified because of them" (Deut. 20:3b). It is also coupled with dismay (Deut. 31:6) and a faint heart (Isa. 7:4). These are the effects and consequences of sinful fear. How dangerous it is to have courage extinguished and faintness of heart strengthened when we have great need of courage! Our peace, perseverance, and eternal happiness depend so much upon it. It is sad to us and dishonorable to religion when we have the hearts of women (Isa. 19:16) instead of men (1 Cor. 16:13). In all ages, we discover that those who manifest most courage for Christ in times of trial are those whose faith surmounts fear and whose hearts are above the world's discouragements.

Basil, bishop of Caesarea, was such a man. This appears in his answer to Emperor Valens, who tempted him with offers of promotion: "Offer these things to children!" When Valens threatened him with grievous suffering, he replied, "Threaten these things to your purple gallants, who give themselves to pleasure and are afraid to die!" This spirit of courage and strength was prevalent among the primitive Christians. They did not fear the faces of tyrants. They did not shrink from the cruelest torments. Their courage was a credit to Christianity. One of Julian's nobles, present at the torture of Marcus, bishop of Arethusa, declared, "We are ashamed, oh emperor! The Christians laugh at your cruelty and grow more resolute by it." Lactantius, an early Christian author, also testifies, "Our women and children, not to speak of our men, overcame their torments. The fire cannot fetch so much as a sigh from them." If carnal fear is ascendant over us, our courage and resolution melt away. When this happens, we might still suffer out of unavoidable necessity, but we will never suffer in a manner that honors Christ and religion.

Effect 5: Apostasy

Carnal fear is the very root of apostasy. It has caused
thousands of professors to faint and fall away in the
hour of temptation. It is not so much our enemies' fury
without as our own fears within that make temptations
victorious over us. Christ dates the beginning of apostasy
from the beginning of fear. "Then shall they deliver you
up to be afflicted, and shall kill you: and ye shall be hated
of all nations for my name's sake. And then shall many be
offended" (Matt. 24:9–10a). When troubles and dangers
come to a height, fear begins to work at a height too. The
critical hour is when fear is high and faith is low, temptation is strong and resistance is weak. Satan knocks at
the door and fear opens it, yielding up the soul to him,
unless special assistance arrives from heaven.

As long as we can profess religion without any great
hazard to life, liberty, or estate, we show much zeal in the
ways of godliness. But when it comes to resisting unto
blood, few will assert it openly. The first retreat is usually made from a free and open to a closed and concealed
practice of religion. We fail to open our windows to show
that we do not care who knows we worship God (Dan.
6:10). Instead, we hide our principles and practices with
all the art and care imaginable. We seek to escape danger
by letting go of our profession. If the inquest continues
and this refuge can no longer protect us, then we give
some open sign of compliance with false worship. We do
it in order to avoid being marked out for ruin. Then, fear

says, "Give a little more ground and retreat to the next security." We comply externally with what we know is forbidden, hoping God will be merciful to us as long as we keep our hearts for Him. In reference to worshipping the Roman gods, Seneca advises, "Let us make an appearance of worshipping them, though our hearts give no religious respect to them." If the temptation hunts us even farther, putting us to a more difficult test and threatening us with death and the loss of all that is dear in this life, we subscribe to contrary articles and renounce our avowed principles. Nothing in the world hazards our eternal salvation as our fear. It is a rock upon which we will make a horrible shipwreck both of truth and peace. This was the case with Thomas Cranmer, archbishop of Canterbury. His fear caused him to go against his own conscience by betraying the known truth. Indeed, there is no temptation in the world that overthrows so many as that which is backed with fear. The love of honors has slain its thousands, but fear of sufferings its ten thousands.

Effect 6: Bondage

Sinful fear places people under great bondage of spirit and makes death a thousand times more terrible and intolerable. We read of some "who through fear of death were all their lifetime subject to bondage" (Heb. 2:15). This means that fear kept them in miserable anxiety and perplexity of mind, like slaves that tremble at the whip which is held over them. Many people live like that—under the lash. The name of death is so terrible, especially a violent death, that they cannot bear to hear it mentioned. Such fear gave rise to the saying: "It is better to die once than to be always dying." Surely, a trembling life is the most miserable life that can be lived. Why?

First, it destroys all of life's comforts and pleasures. No pleasure can thrive under the shadow of this cursed plant. It embitters the comforts we possess in this world. It is said that Democles (an Athenian orator) told Dionysius, the tyrant, that his wealth, power, and majesty made him the happiest man in the world. Dionysius set the flatterer at a table furnished with all dainties. However, he also set a sharp sword, hanging by a single horse hair, over his head. This caused Democles to tremble so much that he could neither eat nor drink. He longed to run from the danger. Dionysius's design was to convince Democles that those who live under the continual terror of impending death are miserable. God threatened His people with terrible judgment: "Wherefore a lion out of the forest shall slay them, and a wolf of the evenings shall spoil them, a leopard shall watch over their cities: every one that goeth out thence shall be torn in pieces" (Jer. 5:6–7a). What a miserable life! They could not leave the city without being seized by lions, wolves, and leopards, which lurked everywhere. Yet, even that is more tolerable than for a person's fear to afflict him continually.

Second, a trembling life destroys the spiritual comforts that flow from God's promises. It also destroys our experience of the promises—the sweetest pleasures we have in this world. As no creature-comfort is pleasant, so no promise is sweet to the person living in bondage to fear. When the terrors of death are great, the comforts of the Almighty are small. In the written Word, there are all sorts of refreshing, strengthening, and heart-reviving promises. By His care and wisdom, God prepared these for our relief in days of darkness and trouble. There are promises of support under the heaviest burdens and pressures: "Fear thou not; for I am with thee; be not dismayed; for I am thy God: I will strengthen thee; yea, I will help thee; yea, I will uphold thee with the right hand of my righteousness" (Isa. 41:10). This promise is able to make the trembling soul shout with the joy of men in harvest, or men who divide the spoil. There are also promises of protection (Isa. 27:2–3; 33:2). In times of danger, these lead us to God's almighty power, placing us under the wings of His care. There are promises of moderation. They enable us to bear the day of sharp affliction (Isa. 27:8; 1 Cor. 10:13). There are promises of deliverance. If our enemies' malice brings us into trouble, God's mercy will assuredly bring us out (Pss. 91:14–15; 125:3). There are promises to bless and sanctify our troubles for our good; our troubles not only cease to be hurtful, but they become exceedingly beneficial (Isa. 27:9; Rom. 8:28). These are the most comfortable promises of all.

Our tender Father provides all these promises for the day of fear and trouble. Because He knows our weakness and how our fear makes us doubt our security, He engages His wisdom, power, care, faithfulness, and unchangeableness for the performance of His promises (Isa. 27:2–3; 43:1–2; 1 Cor. 10:13; 16:9; 2 Peter 2:9). In the midst of such sealed promises, how cheerful should we be in the worst times! We should say as David, "Wherefore should I fear in the day of evil?" (Ps. 49:5a). Let those who have no God to whom they can turn, no promise upon which they can rely, fear in the day of evil! I have no cause to do so. Yet, our fear beats us away from this most comfortable refuge in the promises. We are so scared that we ignore them and fail to draw encouragement, resolution, and courage from them. In this way, the shields of the mighty are cast away.

By a singular providence (aiming at our relief in future distress), God has preserved all the choice records of the saints' experiences in trouble and distress. If danger threatens us, we may turn to the recorded experiences of His people—the mighty influence of His providence upon their enemies' hearts, whereby they showed them favor (Gen. 31:29; Jer. 15:11). There are also the ancient rolls and records of the admirable methods of His people's deliverance. His infinite and unsearchable wisdom contrived these when their thoughts were at a loss (Ex. 15:6; 2 Kings 19:3, 7; 2 Chron. 20:12, 15). There are the recorded experiences of God's unspotted faithfulness, which never failed anyone who dared to trust in Him (Josh. 7:9; Mic. 6:4–5). There are also the records of

His tender, fatherly care for His children, who are His peculiar treasure in times of danger (Deut. 32:10–12; 2 Chron. 16:9; Job 36:7; Ps. 40:17; Isa. 49:16). All these, and many additional helps and supports are made available to us in the day of trouble. But what purpose do they serve if our fear affects us to such an extent that we cannot apply them nor calmly consider them?

Third, a trembling life deprives us of the manifold advantages that arise from a calm and composed meditation upon death. If we could sit down in peace, meditate in a familiar way upon death, and look with a composed mind into our graves without being frightened with the thoughts of death, what a change it would make upon us! What seriousness would those meditations produce in us! What abundance of evil would they prevent in our lives! The sprinkling of dust upon new writing prevents blots and blurs in our books or letters. If we could sprinkle the dust of the grave upon our minds, it would prevent many sins and miscarriages in our words and actions. But promises, experiences, and even death have no profit or advantage when fear puts the soul into a state of confusion.

And thus you see some of sinful fear's mischievous effects.

CHAPTER 6

Remedies for Sinful Fear

We have come to the most difficult part of this book: the cure for sinful and slavish fear. If God applies this cure, we will live at heart's ease in the midst of our troubles and enemies. Like the sun in the sky, we will keep a steady course in the darkest and gloomiest day. But before I come to the particular rules, it is necessary (in order to prevent mistakes) to lay down three important cautions.

First, we must understand that only those in Christ are capable of improving the following rules to their advantage. Christ's greatest argument for extinguishing our fear of those who kill the body is the soul's security (Matt. 10:28). If the soul perishes with the body, or if the soul falls into hell before the body enters the grave, or if he who kills the body also cuts off the soul from the means of mercy and happiness, what can relieve a person against fear of death?

Second, we must not expect a perfect cure for our fear in this life. While there are dangers and enemies, some fear will work in the best hearts. If our faith could be perfected, our fear would be perfectly cured. But while there is much weakness in our faith, there will be much strength in our fear. For those who are naturally timid, who have more of this passion in their constitution, and for those in whom melancholy is a rooted and chronic disease, it will be difficult to remove fear and dejection. But they will be greatly relieved from this tyranny and enabled to possess their souls in much more comfort and tranquility by using the helps and means that follow.

Third, we must not think that the bare reading or remembering of the following rules will suffice. We must work them into ours hearts through fixed meditation and live in the daily practice of them. It is not the explanation of a case to a physician nor his written prescription that cures a person. If he ever expects to be healthy, he must take the bitter and nauseous medication, even if he hates it; he must abstain from unhealthy food, even if he loves it. The same principle applies to the following rules.

Rule 1: Study the Covenant of Grace

The first rule for relieving slavish fear is to consider seriously and study thoroughly the covenant of grace in which all believers stand. A clear understanding of the covenant's nature, extent, and stability, along with our interest in it, will go a long way to cure our sinful and slavish fear.

A covenant is more than a naked promise. In the covenant, God has graciously considered our fears, doubts, and weaknesses; therefore, He proceeds with us in the highest way of solemnity, confirming His promises by way of oath (Heb. 6:13, 17) and seals (Rom. 6:11). He places Himself under the most solemn ties and engagements to His people so that we might take strong comfort from so firm a ratification of the covenant (Heb. 6:18). He has ordered it so that it might afford strong support and encouragement to our faint and fearful spirits in the midst of trouble from within and without. In the covenant, God gives Himself to His people—to be their God (Jer. 31:33; Heb. 8:10). He bestows Himself upon us in all His glorious and essential properties so that we are assured that (in all fears and hardships) He will faithfully perform whatever His almighty power, infinite wisdom, and incomprehensible mercy can afford for our protection, support, deliverance, direction, pardon, or refreshment. God expects us to improve this by faith as the most sovereign antidote against all our fears in this world. "But now thus saith the LORD that created thee, O Jacob, and he that formed thee, O Israel, Fear not: for I have redeemed thee, I have called thee by thy name; thou art mine. When thou passest through the waters, I will be with thee" (Isa. 43:1–2a). "Fear thou not; for I am with thee: be not dismayed; for I am thy God" (Isa. 41:10a).

Reader, if you are within the bonds of the covenant, you will surely find enough there to quiet your heart—whatever the cause of your fear. If God is your covenant-God, He will be with you in all your straits, wants, and troubles. He will never leave you nor forsake you. David used the covenant to encourage himself against all his troubles. "Although my house be not so with God; yet he hath made with me an everlasting covenant, ordered in all things, and sure: for this is all my salvation, and all my desire, although he make it not to grow" (2 Sam. 23:5). He fetched relief, comfort, and salvation out of the covenant. We can do the same. David desired nothing more for his heart's support. Surely, if we understand and believe it as he did, we will desire nothing more to quiet and comfort our hearts.

First, are you afraid of what your enemies will do? We know we are in the midst of potent and enraged enemies. We have heard what they have done, and we see what they are preparing to do. We tremble to think of the bloody tragedies that their cruel hands are likely to perform in this world. But what heroic and noble acts of faith should God's covenant enable you to exert in the midst of these fears! If God is your God, then you have Almighty God on your side. That is enough to extinguish all these fears. "The LORD is on my side; I will not fear: what can man do unto me?" (Ps. 118:6). Your fears come in the name of man, but your help comes in the name of the Lord. Let them plot, threaten, and strike. God is a shield to those who fear Him. "If God be for us, who can be against us?" (Rom. 8:31).

Second, are you afraid of what God will do? Do not fear it! Your God will not do anything against your good. Do not think that He will forget you! It cannot be. A tender mother may sooner forget her nursing child than God will forget you (Isa. 49:15). "He withdraweth not his eyes from the righteous" (Job 36:7a). His eyes are continually upon your wants and dangers. There is not a danger or an enemy stirring against you that His eyes do not see (2 Chron. 16:9). Are you afraid that He will forsake you and cast you away? It is true that your sins deserve it. But He has secured you fully against that fear in His covenant. "I will not turn away from them, to do them good" (Jer. 32:40). Your fear of God's forgetting or forsaking you arises from your ignorance of the covenant.

Third, are you afraid of what you will do? It is common for God's people to propose difficult cases and raise startling questions. These may serve to rouse them out of a false security, force them to try their condition and estate, and make them prepare for the worst. However, Satan usually uses these to a contrary end—to deject, frighten, and discourage them. "If fiery trials were to come, if my life and liberty were threatened, I fear I would not have enough strength to continue in the way of religion. I am afraid I would faint at the first encounter, I would deny the words of the Holy One, and I would make shipwreck of faith and a good conscience at the first gust of temptation. I can hear, pray, and profess, but I doubt I can burn, bleed, or lie in a dungeon for Christ. If I can barely run with footmen in the land of peace, how can I possibly contend with horses in these swellings of Jordan (Jer. 12:5)?" But these fears are groundless—either forged in your own heart or secretly introduced by Satan. God has abundantly secured you against such fears by that most sweet, supporting, and blessed promise: "I will put my fear in their hearts, that they shall not depart from me" (Jer. 32:40b). That is a different kind of fear from the one that startles you. God promises to put it in you—not to shake and undermine your assurance, but to guard and maintain it. This fear is able to vanquish and expel all your other fears.

Fourth, are you afraid of what the church will do? What will become of the ark of God? Do you see a storm gathering, winds beginning to roar, and waves beginning to swell? Are you afraid of what will become of that vessel, the church, in which you have so great an interest? This feeling sense of the church's danger and suffering is an argument for your spirit's excellence. Most people seek their own things, and not Christ's (Phil. 2:21). That being said, it is a sin to fear to such an extent that you sink and faint under a spirit of despondency and discouragement. Many good people are prone to this. I remember an excellent passage in one of Luther's letters to Melanchthon: "In private troubles, I am weaker, you are stronger. You despise your own life, but fear the public cause. But for the public cause, I am at rest, being assured that it is just and true—that it is Christ's and

God's cause. I am a secure spectator of things. I do not worry about what those fierce and threatening papists can do. I beseech you by Christ not to neglect divine promises and comforts. The Scriptures say, 'Cast thy care upon the Lord, wait upon the Lord, be strong, and he shall comfort thy heart.'" In another epistle, Luther writes, "I much dislike those anxious cares, which (as you say) almost consume you. It is not the greatness of the danger, but the greatness of your unbelief. John Huss and others were under greater danger. If it is great, He is great who orders it. Why afflict yourself? If the cause is bad, let us renounce it. If it is good, why do we make Him a liar who bids us to be still? Are you able to do any good by such unprofitable cares? I beseech you (you who in other things are valiant), fight against yourself—your greatest enemy. You put weapons into Satan's hand."

You see, public fears can overwhelm even good people. Certainly, if we were to consider the bond of the covenant that is between God and His people, we would be more composed. By reason of this covenant, God is in the midst of His people (Ps. 46:1–4). When any danger threatened the Reformed church in its tender beginning, Luther would say, "Come, let us sing Psalm 46." Indeed, it is a lovely song for such times. It bears the title: "A song upon Alamoth" (or, a song for the hidden ones). God is with them to cover them under His wings. It is a matter of fact, evident to the world, that no people have been so wonderfully preserved as the church. It has survived bloody massacres, terrible persecutions, and cruel enemies. God has preserved and delivered it, just as He promised (Jer. 30:11). It is obvious to all who will consider it that God's motives for caring for His people have remained the same since the beginning of the world. (1) God's relation to His people is still the same. Abraham, Isaac, and Jacob are in their graves. Those who succeed them are far inferior in grace and spiritual excellence. Yet, says the church, "Doubtless, thou art our father" (Isa. 63:16a). There is the same bond between the Father and the younger, weaker child, as between the Father and the older, stronger child. (2) God's pity and mercy are still the same. They endure forever. His heart yearns as tenderly for His people in the present as it did in the past. (3) The rage and malice of God's enemies are still the same. They act as blasphemously and dishonorably toward God's people today as they ever did. Moses' argument is as good now as it ever was: "Wherefore should the Egyptians speak, and say, For mischief did he bring them out, to slay them in the mountains, and to consume them from the face of the earth?" (Ex. 32:12a). Joshua's question is as good now as it ever was: "What wilt thou do unto thy great name?" (Josh. 7:9b). Oh, if these things were more thoroughly studied and believed, they would relieve many fears!

Rule 2: Consider the Misery of Sinful Fear

The second rule is to consider the mischief and misery that sinful fear produces in this world and in the one to come.

Present Misery

The miseries and calamities that sinful fear brings upon people in this world are unspeakable. It has plunged the consciences of so many poor wretches into deep distresses. It has put them upon the rack and made them roar like the damned in hell. Some have recovered while others have perished in these deeps of horror and despair. In the year 1550, in Ferrara, Italy, God's grace converted Faninus to the knowledge of the truth, wherein he found such sweetness. By constant reading, meditation, and prayer, he became expert in the Scriptures. He was able to instruct others. Although he dared not go beyond the bounds of his calling to preach openly, he was helpful to many through private exhortations. When the pope's officials found out, they arrested him and committed him to prison. When he renounced the truth, they released him. Shortly after, the Lord met with him. He fell into horrible torments of conscience. He was near to utter despair. He was not free from those terrors until he fully resolved to venture his life more faithfully in Christ's service.

As soon as Francis Spira's sinful fear prevailed upon him to renounce the truth, he seemed to hear a dreadful voice in his conscience: "You wicked wretch. You have denied Me. You have renounced the covenant of your obedience. You have broken your vow; hence, apostate, bear the sentence of your eternal damnation!" Immediately, he fell into a swoon, quaking and trembling. Until his death, he affirmed that from that moment he never found any ease or peace of mind. He professed that "he was held captive under Almighty God's avenging hand," that "he continually heard Christ's sentence against him," and that "he knew he was utterly undone with no hope for grace or that Christ would intercede for him to the Father."

In Queen Mary's dreadful days, Sir John Cheek, who had been tutor to King Edward VI, was cast into the tower. They gave him this miserable choice: surrender his life or his liberty of conscience (which is more precious). His friends could not procure his liberty at any lower rate than a full recantation of his religion. He was unwilling to do so until his hard imprisonment, joined with threats of much worse, finally influenced him. His consultation with flesh and blood drew from him a renunciation of that truth which he had so long professed and still believed. As a result, they restored his liberty, but never his comfort. The sense of his apostasy and the daily sight of the cruel butcheries inflicted upon others for their constant adherence to the truth made deep impressions upon his broken spirit. It brought his life to a speedy end.

Our own histories abound with multitudes of miserable examples. Some have been in such horror of conscience that they have chosen strangling rather than life. They have felt an anguish of conscience that has led them to desperate attempts to take their own lives. This was the case with poor Peter Moon. His fears drove him to deny the truth. He fell into such horror of conscience that, upon seeing a sword hanging in his parlor, he wanted to plunge it into his heart. When Francis Spira was near his end, he saw a knife on the table. Running to it, he would have killed himself if his friends had not prevented him. He said, "Oh, that I were above God, for I know that He will have no mercy on me!" He remained about eight weeks (according to one historian) in a continual burning, neither desiring nor receiving anything. He vehemently raged for drink, yet feared to live long. He dreaded hell, yet coveted death. He was in a continual torment, yet he was his own tormentor. He consumed himself with grief and horror, impatience and despair, like a living man in hell. He was an extraordinary example of God's justice and power, and so ended his miserable life.

Surely, it is good to use these dreadful examples to awaken ourselves out of sinful fear. Is there any such misery that we can fear from man's hands? Oh, reader, I believe it; "It is a fearful thing to fall into the hands of the living God" (Heb. 10:31). If you were to feel the rage of a wounded and distressed conscience, like these poor wretches, it would drive you into the same hell on earth.

Future Misery

Unless the Lord overcomes and extinguishes your sinful fear through the fear of His name, it will not only bring you into a kind of hell on earth, but into hell itself for all eternity. "But the fearful, and unbelieving, and the abominable, and murderers, and whoremongers, and sorcerers, and idolaters, and all liars, shall have their part in the lake which burneth with fire and brimstone: which is the second death" (Rev. 21:8). Here, we behold the law of heaven executed upon cowards and renegades, whose fears make them run from Christ in time of danger. Think upon this, you fearful and faint-hearted professors! You cannot bear the thought of lying in a nasty dungeon. So, how will you lie in the lake of fire and brimstone? You are afraid of human frowns. They will die. How will you live among demons? Is man's wrath like God's fury poured out? Is not God's little finger heavier than all the tyrants in the world?

Remember what Christ declares: "But whosoever shall deny me before men, him will I also deny before my Father which is in heaven" (Matt. 10:33). Reader, the time is coming when Christ will break forth from heaven with a shout, accompanied with His saints and angels. The heavens and earth will be in dreadful fire all around Him. The last trumpet will sound. The graves will open. The earth and sea will give up their dead. Your eyes will see Him ascend the awful throne of judgment. His faithful ones, who are not afraid to stand with Him in the face of dangers and enemies, will sit with Him as judges. What will it be like for Christ to disclaim and renounce you forever in the face of that great assembly? What will it be like for Him to proclaim you a delinquent, a traitor, because you denied His name and truth before those who have long since withered like the grass? Oh, how will you endure this? Now, put these two together; consider the terrors of conscience here and its desperate horror in hell. This is a smoldering; that is a roasting in the flames of God's insufferable wrath. This is a scalding drop sprinkled upon your conscience; that is the lake that burns forever with fire and brimstone. Oh, who would choose that suffering out of fear for present suffering which only touches the flesh and is but momentary? Think upon Christ's words: "For whosoever will save his life shall lose it" (Mark 8:35a). Why, out of fear for a trifle, would you prolong a life that ends in the second death? It is nothing compared to what you will suffer from God forever.

Rule 3: Prepare for Future Suffering

The third rule for overcoming the fear of suffering is to prepare for it beforehand. The fear of caution is a good cure for the fear of distraction. One fear cures the other, as one fire draws forth another. "By faith Noah, being warned of God of things not seen as yet, moved with fear, prepared an ark" (Heb. 11:7a). He provided as much for the rest and quiet of his mind as he did for the safety of his person and family. Evil is frightful because it often comes upon us by surprise. Troubles which find us secure leave us desperate and distracted. Presumption of continued tranquility is one of the greatest aggravations of misery. Trouble lies heavy enough when expected, but it is intolerable when unexpected. It is Babylon's lot to suffer the unexpected trials of God's wrath. I wish that only she and her children would be so surprised (Rev. 18:7). It would be good for us to mingle such thoughts as these with all our earthly comforts and enjoyments.

I am at ease in my home, but the time may come when my home will be a prison cell. At present, I see friends' faces full of smiles and honors. Soon, I may only see enemies' faces full of frowns and terrors. At present, I have an estate to supply my wants and provide for my family. But this may shortly become spoil for my enemies. They might sweep away everything and reap the fruit of my labor. At present, I have my life. Oh, how soon it might fall into cruel and blood-thirsty hands! I have no better security for these things than the martyrs had. They suffered the loss of all these things for Christ's sake. Such meditations as these result in a double advantage.

Acquaintance with Trouble

First, they acquaint our thoughts with evils. The more they are acquainted with them, the less they will be startled and frightened by them. We should not think "the fiery trial" is strange (1 Peter 4:12). As it is, our thoughts are like young colts; they startle at every new thing they meet. We cure them by bringing them repeatedly to the thing they fear. Better acquaintance cures this startling humor. The newness of evil, says a learned divine, is the cause of fear. In other words, fear arises when the mind has had no preceding encounter with its object whereby to judge its strength. Fear also arises when the mind has had no example of another person's victory whereby to confirm hope of similar success. As I noted earlier, experience is a kind of armor, a kind of fortitude, enabling the mind to judge and to bear trouble. There are things that children fear only out of ignorance. As soon as these things are known, they cease to be terrible.

I know our minds are naturally reluctant to think upon such harsh and unpleasant subjects. It is difficult to bring our thoughts to them in good earnest. It is difficult to dwell upon them as long as is necessary to achieve this end. We would rather take a pleasant prospect of future contentment and prosperity in this world, of multiplying our days, of dying quietly in our nest. Our thoughts run nimbly upon such pleasant fancies, like oiled wheels. However, when our minds enter the deep and dirty ways of suffering, they have great difficulty. They are like Pharaoh's chariots without wheels. That which is most pleasant is not always useful and necessary. Our Lord was well acquainted with grief. He often thought and spoke of His suffering, and of the bloody baptism with which He was to be baptized

(Luke 12:50). When He perceived the fond imaginations and vain fancies of some who professed to follow Him, deluding themselves with expectations of earthly rest and prosperity, He turned their thoughts to this less pleasing subject—the things they would suffer for His name. Instead of answering a foolish and groundless question concerning who would sit on His right and left hand, He rebuked their folly and asked them a less pleasing question: "Ye know not what ye ask. Are ye able to drink of the cup that I shall drink of, and to be baptized with the baptism that I am baptized with?" (Matt. 20:22). They deceived themselves with such fond and idle dreams. There is other employment cut out for them in the purposes of God. Instead of sitting upon thrones and tribunals, they will be brought before them as prisoners to receive their sentence of death for Christ's sake. Similar thoughts as these would do us a great deal of service.

Preparation for Trouble

Second, such meditations prepare our thoughts to encounter trouble when it comes. Readiness will subdue and banish our fear. We are never as scared of those things for which our minds are prepared. There is a difference between a soldier in complete armor, who is ready for his enemy, and a soldier who is surprised in bed. When his enemy breaks open his door, his clothes are in one place and his weapons in another. It is for this reason that the apostle presses us so earnestly:

"Wherefore take unto you the whole armour of God, that ye may be able to withstand in the evil day, and having done all, to stand. Stand therefore, having your loins girt about with truth, and having on the breastplate of righteousness; and your feet shod with the preparation of the gospel of peace" (Eph. 6:13–15).

We see the benefit of such provision for suffering in Paul's example of courage and constancy: "For I am ready not to be bound only, but also to die at Jerusalem for the name of the Lord Jesus" (Acts 21:13b). The same courage and constancy remained in him when he was going to lay his neck upon the block: "For I am now ready to be offered, and the time of my departure is at hand" (2 Tim. 4:6). The expression signifies a libation or drink-offering. Some people think he is describing how he will die by the sword. His heart was at that place where he could willingly pour out his blood for Christ, as the priests used to pour out drink-offerings to God. It is true that all the meditations and preparations in the world are not sufficient in themselves to carry us through such difficult services. It is one thing to see death at a distance in our imagination; it is another thing to look death in the face. We can behold the painted lion without fear, but the living lion makes us tremble. Although our strength does not come from our own preparation for death, but from God's gracious assistance, yet He usually communicates His assistance through the conscientious and humble use of these means. Let us, therefore, be found waiting upon God for strength, patience, and resolution to suffer as becomes Christians in the serious use of those means whereby He is pleased to work in His people.

Rule 4: Commit Yourself to God

In order to subdue slavish fear, we must commit ourselves and all that is ours into God's hands. This rule is confirmed in Scripture: "Commit thy works unto the LORD, and thy thoughts shall be established" (Prov. 16:3). The greatest part of our trouble and burden in time of danger arises from the unsettledness and distraction of our own thoughts. The way to calm our thoughts is to commit everything to God. This rule must be applied when we face death in its terrible forms and frightful appearances. "Wherefore let them that suffer according to the will of God commit the keeping of their souls to him in well doing, as unto a faithful Creator" (1 Peter 4:19). If this committing act of faith is useful when our thoughts are in the greatest hurry and our fears are in their fullest strength, how much more will it establish the heart and calm its passions in lesser troubles? If you had a trial pending for your estate, and your heart was distracted with cares and fears about the result, yet someone very skilful and faithful assumed responsibility for your case, what a relief it would be to you! If he were to say to you, "Do not trouble yourself about this business, do not lose an hour's sleep over this matter, commit it to me, and trust me with its management," what a burden would be lifted as soon as you committed the matter to him! You would be able to eat with pleasure and sleep in quietness. Committing the matter of your fear to God would give much more ease and quietness. His power, wisdom, and faithfulness are greater than anything found in people.

For this rule to be serviceable to peace and quietness in an evil day, we must understand two things about the committing act of faith.

Its Nature

First, we must understand the nature of the committing act of faith—what it implies. Not everyone can commit themselves to God. Only His people can do it. Yet even they cannot commit themselves to His care and protection any way they choose; they must do it His way. By way of particulars, take note of the following.

First, whoever commits himself to God must do so in well-doing. The apostle limits it to things agreeable to God's will (1 Peter 4:19); otherwise, we would make God a patron and protector of our sins. Let those who suffer according to God's will commit the keeping of their souls to Him in well-doing. We cannot commit our sins to God's protection—only our duties. God is so great a friend to truth and righteousness that He will not take part in sin—no matter how dear you are to Him. If truth lies with your enemies, the mistake is yours. Do not involve God in your errors and failings, much less any sinful designs. You might commit to Him a doubtful case to be decided, but not a sinful case to be protected. It is a vain exercise to shelter any cause under His wings, unless you can write upon it: "Arise, O God, plead thine own cause" (Ps. 74:22a).

Second, whoever commits himself to God firmly believes that all events are in His hands—that He alone directs, orders, and overrules them as He pleases. In all our fear and distress, the committing act of faith rests upon this supposition. "I trust in Thee, Lord. Thou art my God. My times are in Thy hands. Deliver me from the hands of my enemies." Our firm assent to this great truth—that our times are in God's hands—is the reason why we commit ourselves to God. If our times and lives were in our enemies' hands, it would be pointless to commit ourselves into God's hands. Here the contrary senses and methods of faith are as conspicuous as anywhere. Unbelief persuades people that their lives, and all that is dear to them, are in their enemies' hands. Therefore, it persuades them that the best way to protect themselves is to comply with their enemies' will. Faith, on the other hand, tells us that we and all that is ours are in God's hand. No enemy can touch us unless He gives permission. Therefore, our duty is to please Him and commit everything to Him.

Third, whoever commits himself to God resigns his will to God's will. David commits to God that event which made him flee for his life: "And the king said unto

Zadok, Carry back the ark of God into the city: if I shall find favour in the eyes of the LORD, he will bring me again, and shew me both it, and his habitation: but if he thus say, I have no delight in thee; behold, here am I, let him do to me as seemeth good to him" (2 Sam. 15:25–26). In other words, "Lord, the conspiracy against my life is strong, the danger is great, and the result is doubtful. But I commit it into Thy hand. If Thou dost choose to use me in any service, I will see this city and Thy lovely temple again. If not, I lie at Thy feet, for life or death, for the earthly or heavenly Jerusalem, whatever seems best in Thy eyes." This submission to divine pleasure is part of the committing act of faith. Christian, what do you say? Is your will content to step aside so that God's will might take its place? Perhaps you refer difficult cases to God, provided He governs them according to your desires. That is not submission or resignation, but a sinful limiting of, and prescribing to, God. When a beloved child was at the point of death, a friend asked his mother, "What do you desire of God? Do you plead for life or death?" The mother answered, "I refer it to God's will." But her friend persisted, "If God were to refer it to you, what would you choose?" She responded, "Truly, if God were to refer it to me, I would refer it back to Him." That is what it means to commit ourselves and our troublesome concerns to God.

Fourth, whoever commits himself to God renounces all confidence in the flesh. He expects relief from God alone. If we commit ourselves to God, we must "cease… from man, whose breath is in his nostrils" (Isa. 2:22). To trust God in part and the creature in part is to set one foot upon a rock and the other upon quicksand. Acts of faith that give all the glory to God give real relief and comfort to us.

Its Grounds

Second, we must understand the grounds and encouragements we have to commit ourselves and all matters to God. However difficult and frightful the case might be, you can find encouragement in God—your relation to Him and your experience of Him.

First, all that your heart requires to trust God and commit everything into His hands is found in Him. (1) God's power is almighty. He is able to help you. Whatever the case, "Let Israel hope in the LORD: for with the LORD there is mercy, and with him is plenteous redemption" (Ps. 130:7). By "plenteous redemption," he means that God possesses all the stores of power—all the methods, means, and ways to save His people. When they see no way out of their trouble, their hope is God. (2) God's wisdom is infinite. "The LORD is a God of judgment: blessed are all they that wait for him" (Isa. 30:18b). Having mentioned the wonderful preservation of Noah from the flood, and Lot from the brimstone, the apostle Peter concludes (as should we), "The LORD knoweth how to deliver the godly out of temptation" (2 Peter 2:9a). Some people have much power, but little wisdom to manage it. Others are wise and prudent, but lack ability. In God, there is an infinite fullness of both. (3) God's love and tenderness toward His people is transcendent. This sets His power and wisdom at work for their good. Hence, His eyes of providence "run to and fro throughout the whole earth, to shew himself strong in the behalf of them whose heart is perfect [i.e., upright] toward him" (2 Chron. 16:9). Thus, you see how God is in every way the proper object of your trust.

Second, when you consider yourselves, you find encouragement to commit everything to God. (1) You are God's children. To whom do children commit themselves in times of fear and danger if not their own father? "Doubtless, thou art our father," says the distressed church (Isa. 63:16a). Christian, "thy Maker is thine husband" (Isa. 54:5a). Is not that sufficient reason for you to cast yourself upon Him? Does not the child trust his father and the wife commit herself to her husband? (2) You have already trusted God with a far greater matter than your estates, liberties, or lives. You have committed your souls to Him (2 Tim. 1:12). Will we commit the jewel and not the cabinet? Will we trust Him for heaven and not for earth? (3) You have always found Him to be faithful in whatever you have entrusted to Him. All your experiences are good grounds of confidence (Ps. 9:10). Well then, resolve to trust God in everything. Leave the disposal of everything to Him. He has been with you in every strait, want, and fear. He has helped you, and will

He not do so now? Trust in God's wisdom, power, and love, and lean not on your own understanding (Prov. 3:5). The fruit of such submission is peace.

Rule 5: Mortify Your Affections to the World

In order to get rid of your fear and distraction, you must mortify your affections to the world, and to the inordinate and immoderate love of every enjoyment in the world. The more you are mortified, the less you will be terrified. It is not the dead but the living world that puts our hearts into fear and trembling. If our hearts were crucified, they would soon be calmed. It is the strength of our affections that puts so much strength into our afflictions. It is for this reason that the apostle compares the Christian's life to a soldier's life. If he intends to carry himself bravely in fight, he must not entangle himself with the affairs of this life (2 Tim. 2:3–4). It is impossible to follow Christ without first disentangling your heart from the world. The strength of our love for the world is directly proportionate to the strength of our fear. If ever you would rid yourselves of your uncomely fear, you must use God's means to mortify your affections.

First, you must mortify your affections to your estates and possessions in the world. The poorest age produced the richest Christians and noblest martyrs. Ships with much cargo are unsuitable for battle. The believing Hebrews accepted joyfully the spoiling of their goods, knowing that they had "in heaven a better and an enduring substance" (Heb. 10:34). They carried their goods like unconcerned spectators rather than true owners. They rejoiced when soldiers carried off their goods. They were able to do this because their hearts were fixed on heaven and mortified to things on earth. Without a doubt, they esteemed and valued their estates as God's good providence for their comfortable sojourn in this world. Yet they believed the "substance" in heaven was better. As long as it was safe, the loss of their goods did not afflict them. They could bless God for things which for a little time ministered refreshment to them. But they knew they were transitory enjoyments—things that would eventually fly away if their enemies had not taken them. They knew that the "substance" laid up for them in heaven was eternal. They prized and valued earthly things in so far as they moved them towards heavenly things. If Satan turned them into snares and temptations to deprive them of their better substance in heaven, they could easily slight them and take the spoiling of them joyfully. When the ship is ready to sink in a storm, all hands throw the richest goods overboard. No one thinks it is a pity to cast them away. Reason dictates, "It is better for these things to perish than for me to perish." Yet some people refuse to cast these things overboard; as a result, they drown in "destruction and perdition" (1 Tim. 6:9). Demas would rather perish than part with these things (2 Tim. 4:10).

Reader, consider what comfort they can give you, when you look upon them as the price for which you sold heaven and the hopes of glory. If your unmortified heart is overheated with love for them (like Judas's), they will ensnare you.

Second, you must mortify your affections to your liberty and take heed of placing too much esteem upon it. Liberty is a desirable thing to the birds of the air. You can feed them with the richest food, yet they would rather be cold and hungry in their woods than fat and warm in your cages. As sweet as liberty is, there might be more comfort and sweetness in losing it than keeping it. The prison doors might lock you in, but they cannot lock the Comforter out. Paul and Silas lost their liberty, but not their comfort. They were never as free as when their feet were in the stocks. They never ate so well as when they fed upon prisoner's food. God spread a table for them in prison, sending them a rich feast. They had music at their feast too (Acts 16:25). Patmos lies in the Aegean Sea—not far from the coast of Asia Minor. In that day, it was a barren island—a place designated for banished persons. John could not find any earthly refreshment other than what the barren rocks and wild people condemned to live upon it provided. Yet, it was there that Christ appeared to him in inexpressible glory. It was there that he had ravishing visions and saw the whole scheme of providence in the government of this world. He saw the New Jerusalem descending out of heaven like a bride prepared for her husband (Rev. 21:1–4). This turned Patmos into Paradise. No place ever afforded John such comfort as this. Christians must not think there is a strict and necessary connection between liberty and comfort. God may take away the first, but never the second. Let's suppose you are so fond of liberty that you sacrifice truth and a good conscience for it. Will not God make it bitter to you? Has He not already done so to others? They quickly wearied of their liberty. They were glad for an opportunity to exchange it for prison. Oh, what will you do with your liberty when your peace is taken away from the inward man? When God locks up your souls in prison and puts your consciences into His chains and fetters, you will say as the martyr did, "I am in prison until I am in prison."

Third, you must mortify your affections to the inordinate love of life. You must reason yourself into a lower estimation of your life. There are plenty of arguments to assist you. Has it been a pleasant life to this point? You know how the apostle represents it: "For we that are in this tabernacle do groan, being burdened" (2 Cor. 5:4). Should we desire a burdened and groaning life? You also know that "whilst we are at home in the body, we are absent from the Lord" (2 Cor. 5:6). Should you desire a state of absence from Christ? Can you find much pleasure so far from home? You can imagine what you will, but you will never be out of the reach of Satan's temptations, and you will never be free from your own indwelling corruptions. These conflicts do not end until life ends. You are convinced that your soul cannot be satisfied until you are dead. No matter what comforts you enjoy from God in the way of faith and duty, your heart still gravitates heavenward. You also know that you must die and that the time of your departure is near. No death is more honorable to God or comfortable to you as a violent death for Christ. In such a death, you come to Him by choice, not constraint; you give a public testimony for Christ, which is our greatest use. As for the pain and torment, you say as the martyr said, "Whoever takes away from my torment, takes away from my reward." God can make such a death easier to you than a natural death. He will be with you in your extremity and administer reviving cordials.

Oh, work out the inordinate love of life by working in such mortifying considerations upon your hearts! If you apply this point, you will find your pains and prayers richly answered in your hearts' ease and rest in the most frightening times.

Rule 6: Imitate Faithful Saints

In order to subdue your slavish fear, you must strive to imitate the encouraging examples of those who have trod the path of suffering before you. You must look at the cloud of witnesses that encompasses you—a cloud of excellent persons to animate and encourage you (Heb. 12:1). "Take, my brethren, the prophets, who have spoken in the name of the LORD, for an example of suffering affliction, and of patience" (James 5:10). Examples of excellent persons who have broken the ice and beaten the path before us are of excellent use to suppress our fear and rouse our courage in our own encounters.

The first sufferers had the hardest task, for they lacked the helps that they have left for us. Strange torments are most terrible, for acquaintance abates the formidable greatness of evil. They did not know the strength of their enemy; but we fight with an enemy who was defeated by those who went before us. Certainly, living in the last times, we have better helps for subduing fear than anyone has ever had. We hear of the courage and constancy of our brothers in the midst of trials as severe as anything we experience. We read of how they triumphed over all sorts of suffering and torment, and how they were "strengthened with all might, according to his glorious power, unto all patience and long-suffering with joyfulness" (Col. 1:11). We read of how they departed from the courts that censured and punished them, rejoicing that they were honored to be dishonored for Christ (Acts 5:41) and counting the reproaches of Christ greater riches than the treasures of Egypt (Heb. 11:26). We read of their "trial of cruel mockings and scourgings, yea, moreover of bonds and imprisonment: they were stoned, they were sawn asunder, were tempted, were slain with the sword: they wandered about in sheepskins and goatskins; being destitute, afflicted, tormented" (Heb. 11:36–37). In all this, they obtained a good report. They emerged from the battlefield with triumphant faith and patience. It was not the effect of an overheated zeal peculiar to that age, but of the same spirit of courage that is found among Christians in all ages.

When Valens, the emperor, was in a great rage, he threatened Basil with banishment and torture. As to the first, Basil said, "I little regard it, for the earth is the Lord's, and the fullness thereof." As for the second, he said, "What can they do to such a poor, thin body as mine—nothing but skin and bone?" When Eusebius, governor of Pontus, told Basil that he would tear out his liver, Basil replied, "Truly, you would do me a great favor to take out my bad liver, which inflames and diseases my whole body." Christians have put their enemies to shame by smiling at their cruelties and threatenings. Ignatius's love for Christ had so perfectly overcome all fear of suffering that, when they were preparing to throw him to the lions and leopards, he said he longed to be with them, adding, "If they will not dispatch me quickly, I will provoke them, so that I might be with my sweet Jesus."

When we come to later ages, we find more champions for Christ. Luther's courage is trumpeted throughout the Christian world. It would swell this small book too much to note the many instances of his courage for Christ. The same heroic spirit appeared in various people of honor and eminence, who zealously espoused the cause of reformation with Luther. A remarkable example is Ulricus ab Hutten, a German knight. In defense of Luther's cause, he wrote a letter against the cardinals and bishops assembled at Worms. "I will go through with what I have undertaken against you, and I will stir up people to seek their freedom. I neither care nor fear what happens to me, being prepared for either event—either to ruin you to the great benefit of my country, or to fall with a good conscience. So that you may see with what confidence I condemn your threats, I profess myself to be your irreconcilable enemy while you persecute Luther and those like him. No power of yours, no injury of fortune, will change my mind. Though you take away my life, my concern for my country's liberty will not die. I know that my endeavor to remove such as you and place worthy ministers in your room is acceptable to God. In the last judgment, I expect it will be safer for me to have offended you than to have sought your favor."

John, Duke of Saxony, also demonstrated a brave spirit in defending the Reformation. Despising all the offers of court and Rome, and all the terrors of death itself, he appeared against all the devils and the pope in three imperial assemblies, saying openly to their faces, "I must serve God or the world. Which of these two do you think is better?" As soon as Luther's sermons were outlawed, he moved away, saying, "I will not stay where I cannot have liberty to serve God."

Reader, you have a little taste of the zeal and courage of those worthies who have gone before you in the defense of that cause for which you fear to suffer. According to John Chrysostom (archbishop of Constantinople), most people who read or hear such examples are like the spectators of the Roman gladiators, who praised their courage, but dared not volunteer to do what they did. In order to obtain similar courage, you must make use of these famous examples. (1) Use them against the prejudice of surprise. You have good company. You are likely to suffer the same things for Christ (1 Peter 5:9). (2) Use them against the shame that accompanies suffering. In these examples, you see the most excellent people in the world reckoning it their glory to suffer the vilest things for Christ (Acts 5:41; Heb. 11:26). (3) Use them against the torment of suffering. Poor, weak creatures have been carried honorably and comfortably through the most difficult sufferings for Christ. Our women and children, not to speak of men, overcome their tormentors, and the fire cannot fetch so much as a sigh from them. (4) Use them against unbelief toward God's faithfulness. "When thou passest through the waters, I will be with thee" (Isa. 43:2). You have the recorded testimonies of those who have tested this promise. With one voice, they witness for God, "Thy Word is true!" (5) Use them against the sensible weakness of your graces. Are you afraid your faith, love, and patience are too weak to carry you through great trials? Without doubt, many of these people felt the same way. They were people with similar fears, troubled by a bad heart and a busy devil.

They also had their clouds. Yet, God's almighty power supported them. Out of their weakness, He made them strong. Therefore, do not despair. Get your judgment satisfied (Ps. 44:22), your conscience sprinkled (2 Tim. 1:7), and your call confirmed (Dan. 6:10). Like them, exercise faith with respect to divine assistance and reward. Do not doubt that God, who enabled them to finish their course with joy, will be as good to you. Christ has done as much for you as He did for them. He deserves as much from you as from them. He has prepared the same glory for you that He prepared for them. Oh, may such considerations provoke you to show as much courage and love for Christ as they did!

Rule 7: Confirm Your Interest in Christ

In order to get above the power of your fear, make certain of your interest in Christ and your pardon in His blood. The more certain this is, the bolder you will be. An assured Christian is never a coward in suffering. It is impossible to be clear of fear until you are clear of doubts concerning your interest in Christ. Nothing strengthens our fear more than that which clouds our evidences. Nothing cures our fears more than that which clears our evidences. The shedding abroad of God's love in our hearts will quickly fill them with a spirit of glorying in tribulations (Rom. 5:3–5). Once the believing Hebrews understood that they had an enduring "substance" in heaven, their hearts were unconcerned with the loss of earthly comforts (Heb. 10:34). The same should be true of us. Why?

First, the assured Christian knows that his treasure and happiness are secure—beyond his enemies' reach. As long as they are safe, he has every reason in the world to be quiet and cheerful. "I know," says Paul, "whom I have believed, and am persuaded that he is able to keep that which I have committed unto him against that day" (2 Tim. 1:12). That is the reason why he was not ashamed of Christ's suffering.

Second, the assured Christian knows that he loses nothing in death. A Christian makes two bargains. The first is at conversion, when he exchanges the world for Christ in point of love and estimation. The second is at death, when he parts with the world for Christ. Both are rich bargains. Upon this ground, the apostle says, "For to me to live is Christ, and to die is gain" (Phil. 1:21). The believer's death in Christ is unspeakable gain; but if he wants to make the utmost gain, he dies in Christ and for Christ. Consider the following particulars. (1) The believer's living time is his laboring time, but his dying time is his harvest time. While we live, we are plowing and sowing in the duties of religion. When we die, we reap the fruit and comfort of our labors and duties (Gal. 6:8–9). As reaping time is better than sowing or plowing time, so death is better than life for the believer. (2) The believer's living time is his fighting time, but his dying time is his conquering and triumphing time

(1 Cor. 15:55–56). The conflict is sharp, but the triumph is sweet. As victory and triumph are better than fighting, so death is better than life to those who die in Jesus. (3) The believer's living time is his tiresome and weary time, but his dying time is his resting and sleeping time (Isa. 57:2). Here we spend and faint, but there we rest in our beds. As refreshing rest is better than tiring and fainting, so the believer's death is better than his life. (4) The believer's living time is his waiting and longing time, but his dying time is his time of enjoying that for which he has wished and waited. Here we groan and sigh for Christ, but there we behold and enjoy Christ. As vision and fruition are better and sweeter than hoping and waiting, so the believer's death is better than his life.

Third, the assured Christian knows that to die in Christ and for Christ is the best improvement he can make of death. That is evident in a few particulars. (1) Although a natural death has less horror, a violent death for Christ has more honor. For the one who dies united with Christ, the grave is a bed of rest. For the one who dies as a martyr for Christ, the grave is a bed of honor. "For unto you it is given in the behalf of Christ, not only to believe on him, but also to suffer for his sake" (Phil. 1:29). It is a great honor and favor to suffer for Christ. Not everyone who lives in Christ has the honor to lay down his life for Christ. It troubled Ludovicus Marsacus, a French knight, that he was exempted from wearing chains for Christ (as the other prisoners did) simply because of his high position. He resented it as a great injury. "Give me," says he to his guard, "my chains, and make me a knight of that noble order." (2) In a natural death, we submit ourselves to the unavoidable consequence of sin. In a violent death for Christ, we testify against the evil of sin and for the precious truths of Christ. The first is the payment of a debt of justice, owing to Adam's fall. The second is the payment of a debt of thankfulness, due to Christ who redeemed us with His blood. In the first, sin witnesses against us. In the second, we witness against sin. Indeed, it is a great testimony against the evil of sin. We declare to the world that there is not as much evil in a dungeon, bloody axe, or consuming flames, as in sin. We declare that it is far better to lose our carnal friends, estates, liberties, and lives than part with Christ's truths and a good conscience. Ulrich Zwingli said, "What sort of death should a Christian not desire, what sort of punishment should he not want, or what vault of hell should he not choose, rather than witness against truth and conscience?" (3) A natural death in Christ is safe for us, but a violent death for Christ is beneficial for others. By the former, we come to heaven; by the latter, we bring souls to heaven. The blood of martyrs is called the seed of the church. Many grew in confidence because of Paul's bonds. His suffering led to the furtherance of the gospel. The same is true of ours. The Christian is like Samson: he does greater service against Satan and his cause in death than in life (Judg.

16:30). If we die a natural death in our beds, we die in possession of the truths of Christ. But if we die martyrs for Christ, we secure that precious inheritance for generations to come. Those yet unborn will bless God, not only for His truth, but for our courage, zeal, and constancy, by which it was preserved for them and transmitted to them.

In all this, you see that death is great gain to a believer. It is only great gain if he dies in Christ. It is all that, and a great deal more, if he also dies for Christ. Whoever is assured of such advantages in death will feel his fear of death shrink away. He will have life in patience and death in desire. He will not only submit quietly, but rejoice exceedingly to be used of God in such an honorable way. Assurance will call a bloody death a safe passage to Canaan through the Red Sea. It will call Satan, and all employed in such bloody work, Balaams—they bless (rather than curse) God's people (Numbers 22–24). The assured Christian looks upon his death as his wedding day (Rev. 19:7). Thus, it does not make any difference which horse is sent to bring him to Christ (pale or red), as long as he is with Christ, his love. He looks upon death as his day of release from prison (2 Cor. 5:8). It does not matter whether a friend or enemy closes his eyes, as long as he has his liberty and is with Christ.

Oh, give the Lord no rest until your hearts are at rest by the assurance of His love for you and the pardon of your sins! When you can boldly say, "The LORD is my helper," you will quickly say, "I will not fear what man shall do unto me" (Heb. 13:6). If your heart is upright, why should you not attain it? Full assurance is possible or else it would not have been included in the command (2 Peter 1:10). The sealing graces are in you. The sealing Spirit is ready to do it for you. The sealing promises belong to you. But we lack diligence; therefore, we go without comfort. If we would pray more, strive more, keep our hearts with a stricter watch, mortify sin more thoroughly, and walk before God more accurately, how soon would we attain this blessed assurance, and in it an excellent cure for our distracting and slavish fear!

Rule 8: Keep Your Conscience Pure

In order to free yourself from distracting fear, you must be careful to maintain the purity of your conscience and the integrity of your ways in the whole course of your life in this world. Uprightness will give us boldness, and purity will give us peace. "And the work of righteousness shall be peace; and the effect of righteousness quietness and assurance forever" (Isa. 32:17). As fear follows guilt and guile, so peace and quietness follow righteousness and sincerity. "The wicked flee when no man pursueth: but the righteous are bold as a lion" (Prov. 28:1). His confidence is great because his conscience is quiet. The peace of God guards his heart and mind. There are three remarkable steps by which Christians rise to the height of courage in tribulations (Rom. 5:1–4). First, they are justified and acquitted from guilt by faith. Then, they are brought into a state of favor and acceptance with God. They go one step higher to view the coming glory. From there, it is an easy step to glory in tribulations. Once a person obtains the pardon of sin, the favor of God, and a believing view of the coming glory, it is easy to triumph in tribulation. It is as difficult to hinder it as it is to stop a person from laughing when tickled.

Christians have always found it a spring of courage and comfort: "For our rejoicing is this, the testimony of our conscience, that in simplicity and godly sincerity, not with fleshly wisdom, but by the grace of God, we have had our conversation in the world, and more abundantly to you-ward" (2 Cor. 1:12). Their hearts did not reproach them. Their consciences witnessed that they did not make religion a cloak to cover any fleshly design, but that they were sincere in what they professed. This enabled them to rejoice in the midst of suffering. A clay vessel set empty on the fire will crack and break into pieces; so will a formal, hypocritical, and nominal Christian. But those who have real and substantial principles of courage within them will endure the trial, and will be no worse for the fire.

The heathens discovered the advantage of moral integrity—the peace it yielded to the natural conscience in times of trouble. For them, it was like a wall of brass. How much more will godly simplicity and the sprinkling of Christ's blood upon our consciences secure and encourage our hearts! This atheistic age mocks conscience and scorns purity. Let them laugh, for these things will make you laugh when they cry. Paul exercised himself "to have always a conscience void of offence toward God and toward men" (Acts 24:16). It was worth his labor; it repaid him ten thousand fold in the peace, courage, and comfort that it gave him in the troubles of life.

Conscience is the shoulder that must bear the burden. Be careful, therefore, that guilt does not irritate it or sin put it out of joint. Instead of bearing your burdens, you will not be able to bear its pain and anguish. To prevent this, observe these rules. (1) Make sure your heart is in awe of God, every day and in every place. This walking before God will keep you upright (Gen. 17:1). If you speak and live as those who know God sees you, your uprightness will be such that you will not care if the whole world sees you too. An artist came to Drusius (a Protestant theologian) offering to build a house into which no one could see, thereby allowing him to do whatever he wanted in private. "No," said Drusius, "build it so that every one can see." (2) Preface all that you do and design with prayer (Phil. 4:6). Do not involve yourself in anything for which you dare not pray God's blessing. If you dare not pray, you dare not engage! If you cannot send your prayers before it, you may be certain that shame and guilt will follow after it. (3) Be more afraid of grieving God and wounding conscience than displeasing your friends in the world. Consider every temptation to sin, in an attempt to escape danger, to be the same thing as sinking a ship in order to avoid pirates. (4) Consider what counsel you would give others if they were in your situation. Your judgment is most clear when interest is least felt. David's judgment was upright when he judged himself in a remote parable (2 Sam. 12:5–6). (5) Be willing to bear people's faithful reproofs as God's reproving voice. They are no less when duly administered. This will help to keep you upright. It is said of Sir Anthony Cope, an English Protestant, that he shamed no one as much as himself in his family prayers. He desired ministers not to favor his faults, but to tell him and spare him not. (6) Meditate daily upon your dying day. Do everything in relation to it. Keep your peace and integrity, and they will keep out your fears and terrors.

Rule 9: Record Your Experiences of God's Faithfulness

In order to subdue your slavish fear, you must carefully record your experiences of God's care for you and His faithfulness to you in your past danger and distress. You must apply them to your present fears. Recorded experiences are excellent remedies. "Write this for a memorial in a book, and rehearse it in the ears of Joshua" (Ex. 17:14). There were two things in that book: their victory over Amalek and the way they obtained it—incessant prayer. Likewise, you must do two things to secure this mercy for your use and benefit in future fears: you must record and rehearse it, preserve it from oblivion, and seasonably produce it for relief. Experience gives us two special helps against fear.

First, experience abates the terror of suffering and makes it less formidable. Fear says, "They are great waters and will drown us." Experience says, "They are shallower than we think. We can safely cross; others have. We may pass through the Red Sea and not be overwhelmed." Fear says, "The pains of death are inconceivable—sharp and bitter. You know nothing of what the dying feel. You know nothing of what it is like to lie in a stinking prison in continual expectation of a cruel death. It is an unbearable evil." Experience contradicts all these false reports. It assures us that when we are for Christ prisons and death are not what they appear to be from a distance. Oh, what a good report have the faithful given! They have searched and tried these things. They have gone down into the valley of the shadow of death and seen what is in prison and death. Oh, what a sweet account did Pomponius Algerius, an Italian martyr, give of his stinking prison at Lyons in France! In a letter to a friend, he wrote, "I will utter what scarce anyone will believe. I have found a nest of honey in the entrails of a lion, a paradise of pleasure in a deep, dark dungeon. I have found tranquility of hope and life in a place of sorrow and death. Oh! Here it is that the Spirit of God and of glory rests upon us." Blessed John Philpot, an English martyr, in one of his sweet, encouraging letters, writes, "Oh, how my heart leaps that I am so near to eternal bliss! God forgive me my unthankfulness and unworthiness of so great glory. I have so much joy of the reward prepared for me, the most wretched sinner, that although I am in the place of darkness and mourning, yet I cannot lament. I am night and day so joyful, as though I were under no cross at all. In all the days of my life, I was never so joyful. The name of the Lord be praised!" Others have given the signals, agreed upon between them and their friends, in the midst of the flames, thereby confirming that God makes the inside of suffering quite different from what it appears on the outside. Thus, the experience of others abates the terrors of suffering. Your personal experience of God's supports and comforts confirms it.

Second, experience strengthens faith. Your experiences and those of others are like Aaron and Hur, who supported Moses' hands (Ex. 17:12). They support faith while your fear, like the Amalekites, falls before you. What is experience if not the bringing down of the divine promises to the test of sense and feeling? It is our duty to believe the promises without trials and experiments. But it is easier to do so after many trials. Your own and others' experiences, carefully recorded and seasonably applied, are food to your faith and a cure for many of your fears in a suffering day.

Rule 10: Consider Christ's Providential Kingdom

In order to free yourself from sinful fear, you must consider Christ's providential kingdom over all creatures and affairs in this world. Poor fearful souls! Is there not a

King, a supreme Lord, who rules over all? Has not Christ the reins of government in His hands (Matt. 28:18; John 17:2; Phil. 2:9–12)? If we were to study Christ's dominion and the creature's absolute dependence upon Him, it would cure our trust in and fear of others. We would soon realize that they have no power to help us or hurt us, but what they receive from above. In their pride, our enemies are apt to overrate their power. Sadly, we are apt to overrate it in our fear. "Knowest thou not," said Pilate to Christ, "that I have power to crucify thee, and have power to release thee?" (John 19:10). "Do you refuse to answer me? Do you not know who I am?" "Yes," says Christ, "I know that you are a poor, impotent creature, who has no power except what is given from above. I know you; therefore, I do not fear you." But we are apt to accept their boasts as true and to believe their power is as they claim. In truth, Christ sustains all our enemies (Col. 1:17). He binds and limits them (Rev. 2:10). Providence influences their hearts and wills immediately (Jer. 15:11), so that they cannot do whatever they want. God orders their wills, as well as their hands. Jacob was in Laban and Esau's hands. Both hated him, but neither could hurt him. David was in Saul's hands. Saul hunted for him, yet was forced to dismiss him quietly. He blessed rather than killed. Melanchthon and Pomeron fell into the hands of Charles V, yet he treated these great reformers gently, dismissed them freely, not once forbidding them to preach or print the doctrine which he so much hated and opposed.

Oh, Christian! If you will ever rise above your fear, you must settle these things upon your heart by faith. (1) The reins of government are in Christ's hands. Enemies, like wild horses, may prance up and down as though they would trample everyone in their path; but the bridle of providence is in their mouths and upon their proud necks (2 Kings 19:28). (2) The care of the saints is in Christ's hands. He is the Head of the body (Eph. 1:22–23). It is a reproach and dishonor to Christ to fill our heads with distracting cares and fears when we have so wise a Head to consult and work for us. (3) You have lived to this day upon Christ's care. No truth is more evident than this: wisdom beyond your own has guided your ways (Jer. 10:23), power above your own has supported your burdens (Psalm 73:26), and a spring of relief beyond you has met your needs (Luke 22:35). He has performed everything for you. (4) Christ has promised to take care of His people — no matter the circumstances (Eccl. 8:12; Amos 9:8–9; Rom. 8:28). Oh, if we thoroughly believed these things, fear could no more afflict our hearts than clouds could trouble the heavens! But we forget His providences and promises and are justly left in the hands of our own fears to be afflicted.

Rule 11: Subject Your Carnal Reasoning to Faith

In order to obtain a composed and quiet heart in evil times, you must subject your carnal reasoning to faith. You must keep your thoughts under the government of faith. Whoever sets aside the rules of faith and measures things by the rule of his shallow reason is his own problem. If we permit reason to judge all things and derive its conclusions from the appearance of second causes, our hearts will have no rest day or night. Instead, it will keep us in continual alarms.

The best people are prone to measure things by this rule—to judge all of God's designs and providences by reason. In other things, it is the judge and arbiter. We conclude, therefore, that it should be here too. We are prone to believe whatever it concludes and dictates because sense (which gathers intelligence and information for it) backs and befriends it. Luther says, "How wise and strong do its arguments and conclusions seem to us!" This carnal reason is the thing that puts us into such confusion of mind. (1) It quarrels with the promises and shakes our confidence in them (Ex. 5:22–23). (2) It limits God's power and assigns boundaries to it (Ps. 78:20, 41). (3) It draws desperate conclusions from providential appearances (1 Sam. 27:1). (4) It sets us upon sinful courses in an attempt to save ourselves from danger (Isa. 30:15–16). (5) It divides our thoughts and flows into our hearts (Ps. 94:16).

All of these mischiefs arise from our carnal reasoning. This ought not to be the case. Why? (1) Although there is nothing in the matter of faith or providence that is contrary to right reason, there are many things above the reach of reason (Isa. 55:8). (2) Experience frequently confutes the confident dictates of reason. It is made a liar every day. Its fears are proved to be vain and groundless (Isa. 51:13).

Nothing is better for us than to resign our reason to faith, to see all things through the promises, and to trust God over all events.

Rule 12: Exalt the Fear of God in Your Heart

To conclude, in order to subdue your slavish fear, you must exalt the fear of God in your hearts and let it gain the ascendency over all other fears. That is the prescription in our text. Indeed, all the preceding rules are summed up in this one. (1) Does the application of the covenant of grace cure our fears? The fear of God is a part of that covenant and an evidence of our interest in it (Jer. 32:40). (2) Does sinful fear plunge people into distresses of conscience? The fear of God keeps our ways pure (Ps. 19:9). (3) Does provision for evil days prevent distracting fears? The fear of God enables us to make such provision (Heb. 11:7). (4) Do we guard ourselves against fear by committing everything to God? The fear of God drives us to Him as our only sure refuge. They "feared the LORD" and "thought upon his name" (Mal. 3:16). This means they meditated upon His name as their refuge. His attributes were their chamber of rest. (5) Must we mortify our affections to the world before subduing our fears? The fear of God is the instrument of mortification (Neh. 5:15). (6) Do the examples of those who have gone before us help cure our cowardice? The fear of God provokes in us a holy self-jealousy so that we do not fall short of those excellent patterns (Heb. 12:15). (7) Is the assurance of interest in God and pardon of sin an excellent antidote against slavish fear? The fear of God makes us walk in the comforts of the Holy Spirit (Acts 9:31). (8) Is integrity of heart a fountain of courage in evil times? The fear of God promotes integrity and uprightness (Prov. 16:6; 23:17). (9) Does the remembrance of past experiences suppress sinful fear? The fear of God causes us to consider this subject for mutual encouragement (Mal. 3:16). (10) Are God's providences cordials against fear? The fear of God is the character of those persons over whom His providence watches in the most difficult times (Eccl. 8:12). (11) Does trusting in our own reason breed fear? The fear of God severs us from self-confidence and causes us to trust God with all doubtful issues and events. We must sanctify the Lord of Hosts and make Him our fear.

CHAPTER 7

Objections Answered

The pleas and excuses for cowardly fear in days of trouble are endless. It is impossible to answer them all. It is like cutting off Hydra's head—when one is gone, ten more appear. When good people (for I am dealing with such in this chapter) see formidable faces and bloody times approaching them, they begin to tremble. Their hearts faint and their hands hang down with despondency. Their thoughts are distracted. Their reason and faith are so clouded with fear that temptation is exceedingly strengthened. Their principles and professions are brought under their enemies' contempt and derision. If their brothers (to whom God has given more courage and constancy) discern the mischief that results from such uncomely conduct and advise them of it, they have an abundance of pleas and excuses for their fear. They reason the point of suffering in their own thoughts. The matter is debated between faith and fear. Oh, what endless work does their fear impose upon their faith— to solve all the "buts" and "ifs" it raises! I think it is worthwhile to consider some of the principal objections. My hope is that I will prevail with all gracious people to be more upright.

Objection 1: I Am Unaccustomed to Suffering

Some people object, "Suffering for Christ is a strange thing to Christians in this age. We are fortunate to live in milder times—unlike the primitive Christians, and those who struggled in our land at the beginning of the Reformation. By reason of our lack of familiarity with suffering, our fears are excusable."

One fault is a poor excuse for another. Why is suffering such a stranger to you? Why did you not expect it when enjoying the day of peace? Why did you not reckon that such days would come? Did you not covenant with Christ to take up your cross and follow Him? Does not the Word plainly tell you that "all that will live godly in Christ Jesus shall suffer persecution" (2 Tim. 3:12)? Does not the Word declare that "we must through much tribulation enter into the kingdom of God" (Acts 14:22b)? Did you fall asleep in quiet days and dream of untroubled days? Did you expect the mountain of prosperity to remain forever? Did you expect to die in your nest and multiply your days as the sand? Babylon's children dream like that (Rev. 18:7). But Zion's children should be better instructed. How soon may the brightest day be overcast! The weather is not as variable as the state of the church. One moment it is calm (Acts 9:31); the next there is a

storm (Acts 12:1–2). You know that everything on earth
is variable. So, why did you delude yourself with such
fond dreams? As a learned man rightly observes, "The
older the world grows, the drowsier it grows." These are
the days in which the wise and foolish virgins slumber
(Matt. 25:1–13). Surely it is a poor excuse to say, after so
many warnings from the Word and the rod, "I did not
think of such times. I did not expect them."

Perhaps you have considered the possibility of death
and suffering. Your complaint is that you do not live
in a day in which you have the benefit of encouraging
examples of zeal, faith, and patience. In the past, others knew this advantage. They greatly benefitted from
the daily examples of those who suffered. But do you
really believe that nothing but encouragement arises
from witnessing others' trials? At times, it produces
great discouragement. Now God can still use this to
produce zeal in those who follow. In the seventh persecution under Emperor Decius (ca. 250), certain knights
(Ammon, Zenon, Ptolomaeus, and Ingenuus), along
with an elderly man, Theophilus, stood before the tribu-
nal where a Christian was on trial. Seeing him gripped
with fear and ready to fall away, they almost burst
for sorrow. They made signs to him with their hands,
encouraging him to remain constant. Eventually, they
approached the judge's bench professing to be Christians. The judge and onlookers were astonished. Yet the
Christian, standing trial, was encouraged.

Many discouraging spectacles like this were set before the Christians of former ages. It was a great trial for some of them to hear of the fainting of those who preceded them to the judge. In the time of Emperor Valens, the persecutors informed those coming to trial that their fellow Christians had already acknowledged their errors and begged for pardon. They asked, "Why will you stand out so obstinately?" But the Christians replied, "We will remain firm in order to repair their scandal through our greater courage for Christ." These were the helps and advantages they had in those days. Therefore, do not put so much importance upon examples. Their courage flowed from a higher spring and better principle than the company with whom they suffered.

If the experience of others is so great an advantage, then surely you have the best help in this world. You have their example recorded for your encouragement. Therefore, "think it not strange concerning the fiery trial which is to try you, as though some strange thing had happened unto you" (1 Peter 4:12).

This objection is weighed and no great weight is found in it.

Objection 2: I Am Naturally Tender and Sensitive

Some people claim that their nature is soft and tender: "My constitution is weaker; therefore, I am more subject to fear's impressions. Those who have robust bodies and hardy minds can grapple with difficulties better than I can. By constitution and education, I am altogether unfit to grapple with these torments. I do not have enough patience. My heart faints and dies within me whenever I hear of the martyrs' barbarous deaths. I am excused on account of my fear and faint heart."

It is a great mistake to think that the strength of natural constitution can carry anyone through suffering for Christ. It is also a great mistake to think that natural tenderness and weakness, when divinely assisted, cannot bear the heaviest burden that God ever laid on a Christian's shoulders. Our ability to bear suffering does not come from nature, but grace. We know that people of strong bodies and resolute minds have fainted in times of trial. In contrast, what feeble bodies have sustained the greatest torments (Heb. 11:34)! Eulalia of Portugal was young and tender, merely twelve years old. She was raised in an honorable family and was a person of considerable quality. How courageously did she sustain the cruelest torments for Christ! The judge threatened, "Why will you kill yourself? You are such a young flower and so close to enjoying an honorable marriage and a great dowry." Instead of answering, Eulalia cast down the idol and kicked the heap of incense prepared for the censers. When the executioner approached, she declared, "Go to it, hangman! Burn, cut, and mangle these earthly members. It is easy to break a brittle substance, but the inward mind you will not hurt." When one joint was pulled from another, she said, "Behold, oh Christ, what a pleasure it is for those who remember Thy triumphant victories to attain to those high dignities!" Our constitutional strength is not the measure of our spiritual fortitude. God can make the most tender to stand when strong bodies and resolute minds faint and fall.

Are our bodies so weak and our hearts so tender that we cannot bear suffering for Christ? If this is the case, then we are unfit to be His followers. Christianity is warfare. Christians must endure hardships (2 Tim. 2:3). Delicacy is as strange a sight in a Christian as in a soldier. We cannot be Christ's disciples unless we count the cost. We must resolve, in God's strength, to hazard all with Him and for Him. It is pointless to talk of a religion that we do not think is worthy of our suffering.

If, reader, your constitution is so delicate and tender that you are unable to bear the thought of torments for Christ, how is it that you are not more terrified with hell's torments? Those who deny Christ on earth must feel and bear torments eternally. Oh, what is man's wrath in comparison to God's wrath! It is nothing but a flea's bite in comparison to a lion's. Christ asserts as much in Matthew 10:28, "And fear not them which kill the body, but are not able to kill the soul: but rather fear him which is able to destroy both soul and body in hell." Our souls should shrink and shake at the thought of the infinite and unbearable wrath of the great and terrible God rather than at the thought of bodily suffering, which is but momentary.

Your Father's wisdom and tenderness will proportion your burden to your back. He will not overload your feeble shoulders. That which seems unbearable will become easy in trial. God will certainly provide a way of escape or support, enabling you to bear it.

Objection 3: I Am Unable to Withstand Small Trials

Other people point to their previous experience of feebleness and weakness in trials. Their faith and patience failed them. They cannot imagine that they will ever be able to stand in the fiercest trial. "If thou hast run with the footmen, and they have wearied thee, then how canst thou contend with horses? And if in the land of peace, wherein thou trustedst, they wearied thee, then how wilt thou do in the swelling of Jordan?" (Jer. 12:5).

We are strong or weak, great or small, in our trials, according to God's assisting grace. If He leaves us to our own strength in light and ordinary trials, we are overmatched. If He assists us in great and extraordinary trials, we are more than conquerors. At one moment, Abraham can offer up his only son to God (Gen. 22:6). The next, he is so afraid for his life that he acts shamefully, for which Abimelech rebukes him (Gen. 20:9). At one moment, David says, "Though an host should encamp against me, my heart shall not fear" (Ps. 27:3a). The next, he pretends to be insane, acting beneath one enriched with so much faith and experience (1 Sam. 21:13). At one moment, Peter is afraid of a maid's question (Matt. 26:69–70). The next, he boldly confronts the whole council and owns Christ and His truths to their faces (Acts 4:19–20). In extraordinary trials, we can expect extraordinary assistance. God will carry us through the greatest trials—no matter how often we have failed in the smallest.

God's design in permitting us to experience our weakness in lesser troubles is not to discourage us when we encounter greater trials (that is Satan's use). His purpose is to sever us from self-confidence and self-dependence, and to make us see our weakness so that we heartily and humbly bring ourselves to Him in the way of faith and fervent supplication.

Objection 4: I Am Afflicted with Depression

Some people argue that they cannot control their fear because it is a disease (or, at least, a symptom of a disease) with which God has wounded them. A deep and fixed depression prevails upon them to such an extent that the least trouble overwhelms them. If any sad providence befalls them or even threatens them, their fear rises, their hearts sink, their thoughts revolt, their blood boils, and the whole frame of nature is put into disorder. If the Lord permits such dreadful trials to come upon them, they think of nothing but dying at the hand of their fear—even before an enemy's hand touches them.

I know this is the sad case with many gracious persons. I pity those who are afflicted like this. It is a heavy stroke, dismal state, and deep wound. Yet, God's wisdom has ordered this affliction upon His people for gracious ends and uses. He uses it to make them more tender—watchful, attentive, and careful in their ways, so that they may shun and escape as many occasions of trouble as possible. There are higher motives that can make them attentive and tender, yet the preservation of our own quietness is useful in its place. It is a mercy if it (or anything else) is sanctified to prevent sin and promote care in duty. This is a barrier to keep you from straying.

In great trials, that which appears to be a snare might be to your advantage. How? First, these illnesses of body and distresses of mind serve to embitter the comforts and pleasures of this world to you. They make life less desirable to you than to others. They make life more burdensome to you than to others who enjoy more of its pleasure and sweetness. I have often thought that this is one design of providence. In permitting such distresses to seize gracious persons, providence knows how to use this effect for advantage when a call to suffer comes. It may have its place and use under more spiritual considerations: to facilitate death and make your separation from this world easier for you. Although it is a more noble and raised act of faith and self-denial to offer up our lives to God when they are most pleasant and desirable to us upon natural accounts, yet it is not so easy to part with them as when God has first embittered them to us. Your lives are of little value to you now, because of the burdensome clog that you drag behind you. But if you were to increase your burden by so horrid an addition of guilt as the denying of Christ or His truths, you would not know what to do with such a life. It would certainly lie upon your hands as a burden. God knows how to use these things in the way of His providence to your great advantage.

Second, are you a depressed and timid person? If you are saved by grace, it will ultimately drive you closer to God. The greater your dangers, the more frequent and fervent your approaches to Him will be. You feel the need for everlasting arms underneath you to bear these smaller troubles, which are nothing for other people. How much more do you feel this need in deeper troubles that try the strongest Christians to the utmost of their faith and patience?

Third, what if the Lord makes an advantage out of your weakness—to display His power in supporting you? "And he said unto me, My grace is sufficient for thee: for my strength is made perfect in weakness. Most gladly therefore will I rather glory in my infirmities, that the power of Christ may rest upon me... for when I am weak, then am I strong" (2 Cor. 12:9–10). If the apostle's infirmities serve as a foil to display God's grace with brighter luster, he will rejoice in his infirmities. So should you. So then, do not let this discourage you. Nature's infirmity might make death less terrible. It served that purpose for Basil when his enemy threatened to tear out his liver. He thought it a kindness to have that liver, which had given him so much trouble, torn out. It might drive you nearer to God and provide a fit opportunity for the display of His grace in your time of need.

Objection 5: I Am Afraid God Will Abandon Me

Still others object, "What if God hides His face from my soul in the day of my straits and troubles? What if He permits Satan to buffet me with his horrid temptations? What if I sail like the ship in which Paul sailed—between these two boisterous seas? Can I expect less than a shipwreck of my soul, body, and all the comforts of both, in this world and in the one to come?"

As long as the fear of such misery awakens you to pray for its prevention, it is serviceable to your soul. When it only produces distraction and despondency of mind, it is your sin and Satan's snare. The prophet Jeremiah made a good use of such a supposed evil: "Be not a terror unto me: thou art my hope in the day of evil" (Jer. 17:17). In other words, "In the evil day, I have no other place of retreat or refuge than Thy love and favor. Lord, Thou art all I have to depend upon. I comfort myself against trouble with this confidence: if people are cruel, Thou art kind; if they frown, Thou dost smile; if the world casts me out, Thou dost take me in. But if Thou shouldest become a terror to me instead of a comfort, if they afflict my body and Thou dost frighten my soul with Thy frowns, what a deplorable condition would that be!" Improve it for such a purpose as Jeremiah did—to secure God's favor—and it will do you no harm.

It is unusual for God to estrange Himself from His people in times of trouble and to frown upon them when others do. The common evidence of believers stands ready to attest to this truth: they never find more kindness from God than when they feel most cruelty from people for His sake. Consult the whole cloud of witnesses and you will find they have found the truthfulness of that word. "The Spirit of glory and of God resteth upon you" (1 Peter 4:14) seems to allude to the dove, which Noah sent out of the ark. It flew over the water, but could not find anywhere to rest until it returned to the ark. Similarly, the Spirit of glory (from His effects and fruits: cheering, sealing, and reviving influences, which make people glory and triumph in the most afflicted state) seems to hover, to flee here and there over this person and that person, yet He never rests on anyone as long as He does on those who suffer for righteousness's sake. That is where He commonly takes up His abode.

What if it should happen, according to your fear, that heaven and earth are clouded together? It will not be long before the pleasant light springs up again. "Unto the upright there ariseth light in the darkness" (Ps. 112:4). You will have His supporting presence until the Comforter comes.

Objection 6: I Am Unable to Persevere

Some people argue as follows: "What if my trial is long and temptation's siege is tedious? If that happens, I am persuaded that I am lost. I am unable to continue long in prison or torture. I have no strength to endure a long siege. My patience is too short to hold out from month to month, from year to year, as others have done. Oh, I dread the thought of long, continued trials! I tremble to think of the result."

You distrust your own strength and ability, but must you also limit God's? What if you have but a limited amount of patience? Is the Lord unable to strengthen you "with all might, according to his glorious power, unto all patience and long-suffering with joyfulness" (Col. 1:11)? Has He not promised to "confirm you unto the end" (1 Cor. 1:8)? You do not know how much or how long you can bear suffering. You are not to measure your ability to suffer according to your inherent strength, but God's assisting grace. God can make that little speck of patience hold out until deliverance comes. He can enable your patience to work extensively in all kinds of trials and endure to the longest duration and continuance of your trials. Because this is a marvelous thing in your eyes, does that mean it must also be marvelous in God's eyes?

The Lord knows the proper season to come to the relief of your fainting patience. He will assuredly come in that season. "For the LORD shall judge his people, and repent himself for his servants, when he seeth that their power is gone, and there is none shut up or left" (Deut. 32:36). He will see it in the mount of their difficulties and extremities. "For the rod of the wicked shall not rest upon the lot of the righteous; lest the righteous put forth their hands unto iniquity" (Ps. 125:3). God's power watches over your weakness.

Objection 7: I Am Unable to Endure a Violent Death
Finally, some object, "What if I should suffer cruel and exquisite tortures like the rack or fire—the most dreadful suffering that Christians have ever experienced? What will I do? Am I able to bear it? Is my strength made of stone? Death in its mildest form is terrible to me. How terrible is a violent death?"

Who enabled Christians in the past to endure such things? They loved their lives. They sensed pain just like you. They had the same thoughts and fears. Yet God carried them through it all. He can do the same for you. Did He not make the devouring flames like a bed of roses for some of them? Was He not present in the fire? Did He not abate the extremity of their torment? Did He not enable the weak and tender to endure their suffering patiently and cheerfully? Some of them sang in the midst of the flames. Others clapped their hands triumphantly. Up until their final moment in this world, they showed nothing but signs of joy unspeakable. Ah friends! We judge suffering by the outside; it is terrible.

But we do not know the inside of suffering; it can be exceedingly comfortable. When will we do away with our unbelieving "ifs" and "buts," our questioning and doubting of God's power, wisdom, and tender care over us? When will we learn to trust Him in everything? "The just shall live by his faith" (Hab. 2:4). Whoever lives by faith never dies by fear. The more you trust God, the less you will torment yourself.

I am finished. May the Lord strengthen, establish, and settle His people's feeble and trembling hearts through what my weak hand has offered for their relief. Amen.

Some other
Puritan Resources

from
**REFORMATION
HERITAGE BOOKS**

The Inner Sanctum of Puritan Piety:
John Flavel's Doctrine of Mystical Union with Christ

J. Stephen Yuille

978-1-60178-017-1 Paperback, 140 pages

In *The Inner Sanctum of Puritan Piety*, J. Stephen Yuille demonstrates how the doctrine of the believer's union with Christ lies at the heart of the Puritan pursuit of godliness. He analyzes the whole corpus of Flavel's writing, showing how this mystical union is set upon the backdrop of God's covenant of redemption and established on the basis of the person and work of Jesus Christ. Chapters on the nature and acts of this union help readers gain a better understanding of what this union is, while chapters on the blessings, fruit, suffering, evidence, joy, practice, and hope associated with this union show more fully the experiential direction of Flavel's approach to theology.

"This study of John Flavel on union with Christ is indeed a welcome one!"

— Michael A. G. Haykin, Professor of
Church History and Biblical Spirituality
at Southern Baptist Theological Seminary

"Trading and Thriving in Godliness":
The Piety of George Swinnock

Edited and Introduced by J. Stephen Yuille

978-1-60178-041-6   Paperback, 235 pages

In *"Trading and Thriving in Godliness,"* J. Stephen Yuille highlights George Swinnock's conviction that godliness is the primary employment of every Christian. Yuille begins the book by analyzing the influences on, groundwork for, and expressions of piety in Swinnock's life and thought. The remainder of the book presents fifty selections from Swinnock's writings that exemplify his teaching on the foundation, value, pursuit, nature, and means of godliness, as well as its motives.

"Swinnock gives us the essence of Puritanism and J. Stephen Yuille gives us the essence of Swinnock. Here is doctrine and life, vision and devotion, the poetry and the passion of typical Puritan preaching. A first-rate taster of what is available in Swinnock's *Works*."

— Peter Lewis, author of *The Genius of Puritanism*

Meet the Puritans

Joel R. Beeke and Randall J. Pederson

978-1-60178-000-3   Hardback, 935 pages

Meet the Puritans provides a biographical and theological introduction to the Puritans whose works have been reprinted in the last fifty years, and also gives helpful summaries and insightful analyses of those reprinted works. It contains nearly 150 biographical entries, and nearly 700 summaries of reprinted works. A very useful resource for getting into the Puritans.

"As furnaces burn with ancient coal and not with the leaves that fall from today's trees, so my heart is kindled with the fiery substance I find in the old Scripture-steeped sermons of Puritan pastors. A warm thanks to the authors of *Meet the Puritans* for all the labor to make them known."

— John Piper, Pastor,
Bethlehem Baptist Church,
Minneapolis, Minnesota